NOTIONS ON THE CHRISTIAN LIFE: DAILY POSTS FROM PHILIPPINE BILE MINISTRY (2019-2020)

Prayer ,Discipleship, and Sanctification Posts

Prayer Posts

PRAYING GOD'S WILL

Christianity is not always easy in fact _G.K. Chesterton's poignant observation: "The Christian ideal has not been tried and found wanting. It has been found difficult; and left untried."_

But no one who ever truly trusted Jesus Christ to be their Lord and Savior was ever left alone.

Jesus said

John 16:33 " These things I have spoken to you, that in Me you may have peace. In the world you will have tribulation; but be of good cheer, I have overcome the world."

The cup of Salvation will become the cup of Sanctification for the true believer. Its a cup of trembling. Everyone wants the mantle of the prophet, but no one wants the sackcloth that is often required.

Going back to the George Mueller's, DL Moody's, and Amy Carmichael's of the world. They would get hold of God and not let go until they had an answer to a specific prayer. Maybe that is why it took them 3 to 6 hours in prayer time! But once they got that answer, then they would stand on it and keep praying for that, that exact answer.

The answer could be YES, it could be NO, it could be Trust Me, but whatever it was they firmly held onto that. I can tell you that the results in their lives were amazing.

Example: One morning there is no food for the 200 hundred orphans that live in Mueller's orphanages, Mueller prays, and God tells him that it will come for breakfast. So they set the tables and thank God for His provision (3 buildings/dozens of orphans) and there is knock on the door, the baker was baking in the early hours and he felt led by God to bake food for the orphans, the milkman arrives and tells them his cart is broken and he needs to give his milk away because it will spoil and could the orphans use the milk this morning, that was the norm for their lives.

What if the answer is NO? Well this one is harder especially for someone like me. I want what I want, and I am usually sure that God wants the same thing. Once I was working at a small private Christian school and felt like God would use me there, to be in administration and full time ministry, we were even looking at buying a church. But God not only closed the school, I lost my marriage to boot, well that was horrible, how could He say no to my prayers? But after some years, God not only gave me a very amazing Christian wife, but a ton ministry opportunity: worship singing, teaching and even preaching, and now this missionary ministry!!

Example: let us say that you are praying that the Lord would give you a child. Of course you believe that he will, you and your wife have been trying so long, but you are convinced that God's will is this, your own child. But what if the answer is NO, what if you could be even more blessed by adopting a lost child and giving them an eternal blessing! Can we humble ourselves and listen for the hard answers that God might want to send us? Can we? Or are we just sort of stuck on this American idea of physical comfort, wealth, and health? Is it truly a blessing that we have such things, or is it just in our way to that full life in Him?

What if God's will be that your loved one dies, in order to fulfill his Kingdom purposes? What if that person needs to be saved more than they need to continue living in sin? If you knew that the answer was, perhaps your time with them might be better spent? Perhaps.

Be Blessed in Him Today
Philippine Bible Ministry

INTIMATE PRAYER

James 5: 16 Confess your faults one to another, and pray one for another, that ye may be healed. The effectual fervent prayer of a righteous man avails much.17 Elijah was a man subject to like passions as we are, and he prayed earnestly that it might not rain: and it rained not on the earth by the space of three years and six months.

"You must pray with all your might. That does not mean saying your prayers, or sitting gazing about in church or chapel with eyes wide open while someone else says them for you. It means fervent, effectual, untiring wrestling with God. This kind of prayer be sure the devil and the world and your own indolent, unbelieving nature will oppose. They will (try to) pour water on this flame." William Booth, co-founder of the Salvation Army

God wants to spend time alone with you. This was not possible in the same manner under the Old Testament Covenant as it is now under the new. There was a veil between the inner court and the Holy of Holies where God dwelt (of course God is everywhere, but at that point in history God wanted the people to know that His presence was with them in the temple and the tabernacle) The only one who may enter was the High Priest and only once per year on Yom Kippur. It was so holy of ground that if the priest had any unconfessed sin, they would die when they entered His presence. What happened to that whole separation thing?

Well when Jesus dies on the cross the veil was ripped in two from top to bottom

Matthew 27:51 tells us that God removed that veil of separation between himself and the

believer, So now you have access to the Holy of Holies within your own self!! You are the temple of the living God. But, how often do we even think about that. No we just come to the Lord in our 5-10 minute prayers without much thought of His Holiness. No reverence. Well God wants us to spend time with Him, there in this sacred place, and once you get past your requests for daily and earthly needs.

He wants your whole heart, and it begins by entering His presence in reverence of His holiness. Just like that high priest of old, honoring Gods'
Holiness

Be Blessed in Him Today
Philippine Bible Ministry

PRAYING GOD'S PROMISES; BE CAREFUL WHAT YOU ASK FOR.

It is safe to say that as a Christian we can claim all the promises of the New Testament, as we are under that covenant. The covenant of Jesus Christ, that began at the cross and was attested to at the resurrection, and was completed at the ascension, when Jesus sat at the right hand of God, when He entered His kingdom on that day.

But it can get a bit tricky when we try and claim every promise of the Old Testament, as we are not Jews, those promises were made to the Jews. Yes, some of them are for all believers, which is why you need to be careful.

I will give a glaring example of that here today.

This is the one that many will claim for America today, especially on the "National Day of Prayer"

2 Chronicles 7:14 If My people who are called by My name humble themselves and pray and seek My face and turn from their wicked ways, then I will hear from heaven, will forgive their sin and will heal their land.

I do not know how many times I prayed for that, sincerely wanted the Lord to heal America.

Yes, if you read these posts you know that I already addressed this section of scripture; Her is a brief recap of that:

1.Gods people were the Jews; this was prayed by Solomon at the dedication of the temple. It is a promise to them.

2. It cannot be a promise to believers today, though we are also His people called Christians (by His name) because we do not have land. Our home is in truth; heaven, and not USA or France, or any country. So it does not apply; though it sure sounds good

Then as I was reading my Bible a few days ago and I read the second part of this promise:

You better sit down, because you have forgot to realize exactly what you were agreeing to when you prayed that promise. You know that in the Old Testament that the promises were a two-edged sword:

The good part was this prayer that we love so much: If my people do this, then I will do that for them.

Now let's look at the second part of that promise. It is part of the same prayer, a promise from God.

Do you want to claim this?

2 Chronicles 7:19 "But if you turn away and forsake My statutes and My commandments which I have set before you, and go and serve other gods, and worship them, 20 then I will uproot them from My land which I have given them; and this house which I have [g]sanctified for My name I will cast out of My sight, and will make it a proverb and a byword among all peoples.

Pay attention to God's word, and do not be so fast to grab all the good stuff, unless of course you accept the entire promise bones and all!

It clearly says that If my people *do not* humble themselves and turn that God will pretty much destroy them. So Let me put this in focus for you, in modern day simple words:

If my people humble themselves and turn from wickedness, I will heal their land, if they do not and continue to worship other things (like wealth, fame, money, etc.) then I will destroy them and remove them from their land.

I am glad that we are not under the Old Covenant that this promise was made under. Because we see many in "The Church" that are

NOTIONS ON THE CHRISTIAN LIFE:

worshiping these things, you do not want to ask God for that, do you?

This promise is clearly not about New Testament Christians. Do you see that? In the Old testament that was the deal. You do well and God blesses, you fall away and He removes the blessing.

In the New Covenant, while there are consequences for things, we as Christians have the Grace of God. Though there are no guarantees that this nation nor any other will remain. His people will remain His people.

So, if you see a promise from the Old Testament, be sure to check it out. You need to study God's word before you can actually use it correctly.

Having said all of this; many of the Old Testament promises are for us. Many of the promise found in the book of Isaiah are for Christians today. The key is if the promise is about Christ or not? If it is not actually a prophecy about Christ as we find in Isaiah, then it is usually a promise for Israel, we are not Israel. We are the new man, not to have all their promises, but chosen for Salvation. The other way to know if the OT promises are for the Christian today: if it is also included in the new Testament. The verse about God never leaving nor forsaking us is found in Hebrews 13 as well as Joshua 1.

I will leave you with a couple of my favorite New Testament Promises:

Romans 8:38-39 For I am persuaded that neither death nor life, nor angels nor principalities nor powers, nor things present nor things to come, nor height nor depth, nor any other created thing, shall be able to separate us from the love of God which is in Christ Jesus our Lord.

John 3:16 For God so loved the world, that he gave his only begotten Son, that whosoever believes in him should not perish, but have everlasting life.

Be Blessed IN Him Today
Philippine Bible Ministry

BASICS: PRAYER TIPS FROM EM BOUNDS

James 5:16 Confess *your* trespasses to one another, and pray for one another, that you may be healed. The effective, fervent prayer of a righteous man avails much.

Edward McKendree Bounds was a Methodist minister, revivalist, author and lawyer.

Unsuccessful in the California gold rush of 1849, E.M. Bounds returned home to Missouri and became the state's youngest practicing attorney at age 19. In his early twenties he was deeply impacted by the Third Great Awakening, and at age 24 he was ordained for ministry. During his lifetime he pastored churches, traveled as an evangelist, served as a Civil War chaplain, edited a Christian periodical and was a devoted husband and father. But E.M. Bounds is best known for prayer. His daily habit was to spend the time between 4 am and 7 am praying. His writings on prayer are widely acclaimed to be among the finest of any author before or since.

Tip 1: time spent with God is the secret of all successful praying.

While many private prayers, in the nature of things, must be short; while public prayers, as a rule, ought to be short and condensed; while there is ample room for and value put on ejaculatory prayer -- yet in our private communions with God time is a feature essential to its value. Much time spent with God is the secret of all successful praying. Prayer which is felt as a mighty force is the mediate or immediate product of much time spent with God. Our short prayers owe their point and efficiency to the long ones that have preceded them.

The short prevailing prayer cannot be prayed by one who has not prevailed with God in a mightier struggle of long continuance. Jacob's victory of faith could not have been gained without that all-night wrestling. God's acquaintance is not made by pop calls. God does not bestow his gifts on the casual or hasty comers and goers. Much time with God alone is the secret of knowing him and of influence with him. He yields to the persistency of a faith that knows him. He bestows his richest gifts upon those who declare their desire for and appreciation of those gifts by the constancy as well as earnestness of their importunity.

Prayer Tips from EM Bounds: Tip 2. our purpose is to impress on our minds the necessity of being much alone with God...

Christ, who in this as well as other things is our Example, spent many whole nights in prayer. His custom was to pray much. He had his habitual place to pray. Many long seasons of praying make up his history and character. Paul prayed day and night. It took time from very important interests for Daniel to pray three times a day. David's morning, noon, and night praying were doubtless on many occasions very protracted. While we have no specific account of the time these Bible saints spent in prayer, yet the indications are that they consumed much time in prayer, and on some occasions long seasons of praying was their custom.

We would not have any think that the value of their prayers is to be measured by the clock, but our purpose is to impress on our minds the necessity of being much alone with God; and that if this feature has not been produced by our faith, then our faith is of a feeble and surface type.

Tip 3: Spend enough time

Luther said: "If I fail to spend two hours in prayer each morning, the devil gets the victory through the day.

The men who have most fully illustrated Christ in their character, and have most powerfully affected the world for him, have been men who spent so much time with God as to make it a notable feature of their lives. Charles Simeon devoted the hours from four till eight in the morning to God. Mr. Wesley spent two hours daily in prayer. He began at four in the morning. Of him, one who knew him well wrote: "He thought prayer to be more his business than anything else, and I have seen him come out of his closet with a serenity of face next to shining."

John Fletcher stained the walls of his room by the breath of his prayers. Sometimes he would pray all night; always, frequently, and with great earnestness. His whole life was a life of prayer. "I would not rise from my seat," he said, "without lifting my heart to God." His greeting to a friend was always: "Do I meet you praying?"

_Luther said: "If I fail to spend two hours in prayer each morning, the devil gets the victory through the day. I have so much business I cannot get on without spending three hours daily in prayer." He ha_d a motto: "He that has prayed well has studied well."

Be Blessed in Him Today
Philippine Bible Ministry

CHURCH ACTIVITY: A SUBSTITUTE FOR PRAYER?

Activity in itself is not strength. What we see with the eye in a church is often much running around. The colt is much more active than the mother, but she is the strength of the team quietly pulling the load Enthusiasm and showmanship is more actively seen than faith, but it cannot move mountains, nor change lives. It is true that we can only see activity with our natural eyes.

And we do expect to see surface growth in the church

But any true growth or power is unseen and found in the deep roots of prayer and faith. Those roots are unseen.

Isaiah 40:31

But those who wait on the LORD. Shall renew their strength; They shall mount up with wings like eagles, they shall run and not be weary, They shall walk and not faint.

All true Godly activity is the result of this waiting on Him.

There may be much activity at your church, much of it may be done by tradition or created by enthusiasm, or the product of weakness of the flesh producing short lived forces that are only Christian in appearance. Activity generally in churches can tend to lead to the neglect of truly deep and fervent prayer.

Are we too busy with Gods "work" to take time to commune with Him?

All this work may be blindness without the cultivation and the maturity of the graces of prayer.

You can tell the strength of a church by their prayer meetings, if in fact they even have a separate prayer meeting.

Be Blessed in Him Today
Philippine Bible Ministry

"If you do not spend much time with the Lord in prayer. What do you think will happen when you have eternity with Him?"

TIME FOR PRAYER

Prayer: It has been said the *Martin Luther once said. "I have so much to do that if I didn't spend at least 3 hours in prayer a day, I would never get it done"* Sounds like hyperbole to us. But if you look at some of the giants of the faith; DL Moody, William Booth, Amy Carmichael, Charles Spurgeon, etc., you would find that this was the minimum time they spent before God in prayer.

How can we possibly spend even one hour in prayer with our busy schedules? 24 hours in a day; typically, 8 for work, 8 for sleep, 8 for? OK 8 hours of our time. Of course with family stuff maybe more like 2 or 3; 2 or 3 hours in the day for personal stuff.
It is approximated that the average American spends up to 8 hours per day on their devices (phones, laptops, games)

The Lord has told me specifically to redeem my time, One day I will stand before Him to give an account of how I spent my life, it's called the Judgement (or Bema) seat of Christ:
2 Corinthians 5:10 "For we must all appear before the judgment seat of Christ; that every one may receive the things done in his body, according to that he hath done, whether it be good or bad."

At that time all the earthly things that we spent our time on will be burnt up as hay and stubble, not eternal value. Think on it this way, did Jesus die on the cross so that you could spend your "free" time washing your mind in amusement? Now there is nothing wrong with amusement, I think we all need a break from the world to refresh, But the thing is,, as a believer I had spent way too much time watching mindless stuff. Thanks to my wife who did not grow up watching tv. The Lord used her to convict me that I was wasting much of my life away watching Sci Fi.....So I asked Him to redeem my time.

Here is my goal: spend as much time in prayer as I do engaged in secular stuff on tv, movies, games, etc...
I am not quite there yet, but thanks be to the Lord, I now have a prayer list that grows each day.. If I even pray for one hour per day, I will feel like I have started to actually pray.

Why so long? Isn't prayer just talking to God, I do that all the time. Yes to a degree that is true, but once again, if you are concerned about the 1 million or so who perish each week without the Lord, or all the needs in your immediate family, well I think that we need to learn how important this is, Get a hold of God means to spend this time, not just in asking for comforts, health, and wealth, But to listen to Him!!

He has a specific purpose for every believer on the planet, You have been chosen for something. And just so you know, God is big, and I believe that if the entire body of Christ would humble themselves and seek Him like this, that the world would be changed.

But do not let me interrupt your Netflix (or football) time. Be blessed; I am praying for you....

BeBlessedinHimToday   Philippine Bible Ministry

PRAYER THAT GETS RESULTS:

From EM Bounds "genuine authentic prayer must be definite and free of doubt"

That is quite a statement. I have earlier said that we all need to learn to pray. This definitely includes me.

I highly recommend that you look at the lives of some of the past great prayer warriors for insight on this.

"Robber of the Cruel Streets" is an amazing biographical documentary on the life of George Mueller. A great man of prayer and faith. During his life he received what can be said in today's equivalent to be millions of dollars in donations, YET HE NEVER ASKED FOR ONE CENT! That is, he never asked a human, He lived his life in constant prayer and the Lord supplied all of the needs for his ministry. (He created homes for hundreds of street orphans) At the age of 70 George was convinced to give up his orphanages and preach, So at 71 he began to preach around the world, Kind of old we might say, Well at this time he also began to read his Bible 4 times per day, in addition to his 3 hours minimum daily prayer, One time there was a storm and the captain told him that they would be delayed and he would miss his preaching engagement. :" I have never missed an engagement He told the captain, let us go down and pray" When he and the captain were in the cabin Mueller prayed a prayer of faith, then the captain began his prayer" If it be your will" Mueller stopped him right there, "its ok;" he said, "You do not believe it will happen, but God has already answered my prayer" Well imagine the captains shock when he found the storm had cleared and they made port on time.

This kind of prayer is what I am after, these folks prayed God's will, and they did not let go of the Lord until they received an answer, even a promise. it might be coincidence to the unbeliever, but the lives of Mueller, DL Moody, Spurgeon, Hudson Taylor, etc.. Would argue the fact, these prayers were effective because of belief and because these did not let go until they had an answer.

So Lord teach me to pray like that...Not to let go until I know that you have heard, Why should we just say that those past were just amazing and now we do not have that kind, of what? That kind of faith? That kind of God? No God has not changed.

DL Moody: His friend ***Henry Varley said, "The world has yet to see what God can do with and for and through and in a man who is fully and wholly consecrated to Him."***

Do any of us want to be such a person?
or do we just want God to be with us, kind of holding us together as we survive this world,
In the words of Casting Crowns "we were meant to ***Thrive!"***

Be Blessed in Him Today
Philippine Bible Ministry

FAMOUS INTERCESSORS IN PRAYER

Intercession is prayer that pleads with God for the needs of others. But it is also much more than that. Intercession involves taking hold of God's will and refusing to let go until His will comes to pass.

Intercession is warfare -- the key to God's battle plan for our lives. But the battleground is not of this earth.

The Bible says, in **Ephesians 6:12 For we do not wrestle against flesh and blood, but against principalities, against powers, against the rulers of [a]the darkness of this age, against spiritual hosts of wickedness in the heavenly places.**

Here are just a few examples of intercessory prayers

Moses pleaded with God to save the nation of Israel, after the people had already committed great sin against the Lord. Moses pleaded for them. He even told God to take his own life if he would not spare the people.

Exodus 32:31 Then Moses returned to the Lord and said, "Oh, these people have committed a great sin, and have made for themselves a god of gold! 32 Yet now, if You will forgive their sin—but if not, I pray, blot me out of Your book which You have written."

Pretty strong sentiments from one of the few men that actually walked daily with God.

Perhaps more than anything else, John Knox is known for his

prayer "Give me Scotland, or I die." Knox's prayer was not an arrogant demand, but the passionate plea of a man willing to die for the sake of the pure preaching of the gospel and the salvation of his countrymen. This was the heart of a true intercessor.

Paul, the Apostle also had a huge heart for his people the Jews. He also prayed for their salvation in the book of Romans

Romans 9:3 For I could wish that I myself were accursed from Christ for my brethren, my [a]countrymen according to the flesh,

Many of the prophets also were great intercessors for their people. Here is Ezra the profit also pleading mercy for the Jews

Ezra 9: 10 And now, O our God, what shall we say after this? For we have forsaken Your commandments, 11 which You commanded by Your servants the prophets, saying, 'The land which you are entering to possess is an unclean land, with the uncleanness of the peoples of the lands, with their abominations which have filled it from one end to another with their impurity. 12 Now therefore, do not give your daughters as wives for their sons, nor take their daughters to your sons; and never seek their peace or prosperity, that you may be strong and eat the good of the land, and leave it as an inheritance to your children forever.'

And the prophet Daniel did likewise:

Daniel 9: 16 "O Lord, according to all Your righteousness, I pray, let Your anger and Your fury be turned away from Your city Jerusalem, Your holy mountain; because for our sins, and for the iniquities of our fathers, Jerusalem and Your people are a reproach to all those around us. 17 Now therefore, our God, hear the prayer of Your servant, and his supplications, and for the Lord's sake [a]cause Your face to shine on [b] Your sanctuary, which is desolate.

Jesus of course always interceded and continues to do so this day.

Romans 8:34 Who is he who condemns? It is Christ who died, and furthermore is also risen, who is even at the right hand of God, who also makes intercession for us.

John 17: 20 "I do not pray for these alone, but also for those who will believe in Me through their word; 21 that they all may be

one, as You, Father, are in Me, and I in You; that they also may be one in Us, that the world may believe that You sent Me.

Jesus the ultimate intercessor; and by the way, He actually did give His life for us. Now that is intercession!
Who will you intercede for today?

Be Blessed in Him Today
Philippine Bible Ministry

MINISTRY OF PRAYER

How important is prayer? Our prayers are often limited to brief list of things we want, sometimes for others, yet we do not spend too much time in prayer.

Did you know that no major work of God has ever happened without prayer?

• The creation of the universe: since prayer is communion or communication with God; that includes the creation of the universe. Look it up in Genesis 1, it's a conversation with the Trinity, the Spirit Hovered, the Father Spoke, and Jesus (The Word) created.
• Salvation: Gods people, Israel, prayed for the Messiah
• Pentecost: The Apostles prayed in the upper room for 10 days and then the Holy Spirit created the church.

Jesus said in

Matthew 21:13 (KJV) : And said unto them, It is written, My house shall be called the house of prayer; but ye have made it a den of thieves.

Not a house of teaching, Not a house of preaching, Not a house of fellowship, Not even a house of Love.............. **But a house of prayer**

We wait for God to move. But He is waiting for us to move in prayer: many are just sitting in their Christianity, just waiting for the Rapture, or just waiting to go home to the Lord, but do not really lean into the Lord much

Did you know that every major revival was precede by travailing prayer. Travailing prayer is when the Lord breaks your heart by the state of the world around you, and then you fall down an pray that God would do a work,, And you cry out to the Lord. You trav-

ail in prayer, for hours, days, even months, Then what happened was the Holy Spirit poured out His power on the people. Churches were filled day and night, folks were falling on their knees in the streets asking because of their sinful hearts. It might sound strange to the typical church going person, But look it up:
• The Great Awaking came in three waves from early 18th century to early 20th century
• 1904 Welsh Revival
• Korean Revival of 1907

There are more, some are smaller located in small towns or even in small churches; the one thing they all have in common is that it usually starts with one or two persons that are broken by the world around them. And they reach out and grab the Lord in prayer. And God answers.
Read the book Fresh Wind, Fresh Fire by Jim Cymbala, a true story about the revival that took place in the founding of the Brooklyn Tabernacle. Its an amazing story that might just wake up a few.
This type of prayer is in addition to the ongoing conversation I have with the Lord most all of the day. It is a different type of prayer, focused and travailing. (I like that word, travailing)
My idea is to replace the unfruitful hours I watch TV with prayer and time in Gods word, I want to close to Him and I want all He has for me, so I want to learn to commune with Him. I try to find a quiet time each day,
After all, if you read about the great men and women of faith from the past (Martin Luther,DL Moody, Charles Spurgeon, Amy Carmichael, John Wesley, etc.) You will see that they spent hours in prayer and God did great things through them, That is all He is waiting for , those folks were not different or better than we can be, God is waiting for us to give Him the time that He deserves. Or do you think that binging that favorite program, or watching 2 or 3 football games each weekend is going to advance God's Kingdom?
Jesus spent hours with the Lord alone, then He poured Himself out to the world. That is the model for us, if we dare to lean into it.

God will give you as much of Himself as you give Him of yourself. " The potency of prayer hath subdued the strength of fire; it hath bridled the rage of lions, hushed anarchy to rest, extinguished wars, appeased the elements, expelled demons, burst the chains of death, expanded the gates of heaven, assuaged diseases, repelled frauds, rescued cities from destruction, stayed the sun in its course, and arrested the progress of the thunderbolt" Chrysostom

Start by praying about all of this, ask the Lord if He wants you to spend this kind of time in prayer. Ask Him if He wants your heart to be broken by the things that break His heart.

Like for example the one million souls going to eternal damnation each week.

BeBlessedinHimToday   Philippine Bible Ministry

SOME DIRECTION FOR PASTORS/MINISTERS

Acts 26:16 But rise and stand on your feet; for I have appeared to you for this purpose, to make you a minister and a witness both of the things which you have seen and of the things which I will yet reveal to you.

This was Paul's first commission into the ministry. It was given directly to Him from the Lord Jesus Christ. He was called to give witness to the things that God had showed him and would show him

This is a call to all ministers; preachers, Bible teachers, missionaries, evangelists, etc.

We are to tell the world what the Lord has done for us. And all the things that God continues to show us. These things will of course depend on how much time the "minister" (believer) is spending with the Lord. And how they spend that time. Prayer. Bible study. (not just reading the Bible, but actually studying it) Communing listening worship.

What God showed me during my salvation event, that He is Lord over the demonic forces of the world. That He loves me and that He would and did go to great lengths to save me.

Then almost immediately after I was saved God changes me radically. So he showed me that

His word was true

What He continues to show me. Depends on my time with Him. He is showing me that I can be sanctified as I lean into Him. He is showing me sound doctrine. He is showing me that I need to give and live my life for Him.

Acts 26:17 I will deliver you from the Jewish people, as well as from the Gentiles, to whom I now send you,

The original language says the people and the nations. In other words, we have nothing to fear from people or even nations as we step out into the call that God has on our lives. Nothing to fear from those that would be against us

Acts 26:18 to open their eyes, in order to turn them from darkness to light, and from the power of Satan to God, that they may receive forgiveness of sins and an inheritance among those who are sanctified by faith in Me.'

To tell the world things which will open their eyes spiritually; the truth of sin and darkness and the light and salvation that Jesus offers us. That this world is essentially darkness. The glitter of Vegas, the excitement of entertainments. These seem to shine bright. But in reality they hide the darkness that is in all things that are not of Him.

But those that receive Him will inherit everlasting life   Amen to that...

BeBlessedinHimToday   Philippine Bible Ministry

DISCIPLESHIP/ SANCTIFICATION POSTS

(Part 3 of the series)

TRACK WALKER

"Smart men walked on the moon, daring men walked on the ocean floor, but wise men walk with God." Leonard Ravenhill

Ephesians 2:10 "For we are His creation, created in Christ Jesus for good works, which God prepared ahead of time so that we should walk in them."

About one hundred years ago, most everyone rode the train. The tracks had to be kept in good condition because they were used so much and so many folks relied on them

The trains were the life blood of the nation. They would divide the rails into maybe 5 mile sections, they would have one person in charge of one section, he would get the workers and send them out each day to repair different sections of tracks as needed. The way they knew which places to repair was because of the track walkers. There was one track walker for every 5-mile section of track section and each day that person would walk the track to to see if they needed new spikes, new rails, or whatever repairs they might need. This person had to be in good shape, and they had to have good feet and good shoes.

Our walk with the Lord is like that in some ways. I suppose that the whole track are the lives of every believer on earth; the particular 5-mile section of track is our own lives, or you might better say; our walk with the Lord.

I suppose that the Holy Spirit oversees keeping us in good repair, but we also have our part,Our part is that of the track walker, we should daily be inspecting our lives to see where we might need the attention of the Holy Spirit.

Ephesians 5: 15 See then that you walk circumspectly, not as

fools, but as wise,

Then we ask the Lord to work on those sections. We do not do the work, it's God's work in us

However, we better be involved daily in it. Daily asking Him to point out these things in us

Psalm 139: 23 Search me, O God, and know my heart; Try me, and know my anxieties; 24 And see if there is any wicked way in me, And lead me in the way everlasting.

Do you know what could happen when a track is in bad repair? The entire train, which could be like our salvation or at least our soul's usefulness to the Lords work. It can all be derailed in an instant.Like the pastor who stumbles in adultery, a tragedy like that.

Stay alert and ask Him to help you with your daily track walking

Be Blessed in Him Today
Philippine Bible Ministry

SIDE NOTE TO CHRISTIANS: JESUS IS ALIVE! ARE YOU?

"Jesus Christ did not come into the world to make bad men good. He came to make dead men alive!" Leonard Ravenhill

Ephesians 2:1 And you He made alive, who were dead in trespasses and sins,

Christianity is the only religion that declares that God will come and live inside of you when you accept His sacrifice and ask Him to be your Lord and Savior. No other religion offers such an intimate relationship with the creator of the universe.

The Church needs to start acting like the Bride of Christ, instead of the Widow of Christ

There are probably one million lost souls dying without Christ each week!!

Yet many Christians continue to stay stuck in this soft and lovely type of Christianity, that just prays for comfort and sits around waiting for the rapture.

Think of Christ in Gesthmane, sweating drops of blood, while he realizes what He is about to suffer, not just the cross but separation from the Father. Then He stops and considers your life and He thinks to Himself, well I guess its all worth it if John gets to go on a cruise with Mercy Me in 2019! Or Betty gets to go to Israel in 2020. No, He thought of the sinners that needed Him! The millions or billions that still do need Him.

Then as you think of Him on that cross you decide what you will do with your life??

Good preachers comes to disrupt our lives for Christ , not to make us feel good, You get that at Disneyland.

Be Blessed in Him Today
Philippine Bible Ministry

WAKE UP YOU SLEEPERS

Ephesians 5:13 But all things that are exposed are made manifest by the light, for whatever makes manifest is light. 14 Therefore He says: "Awake, you who sleep, Arise from the dead, And Christ will give you light." 15 See then that you walk circumspectly, not as fools but as wise, 16 redeeming the time, because the days are evil. 17 Therefore do not be unwise, but understand what the will of the Lord is.

Interesting section of scripture here. The sleeper that Paul talks about here are those in the church at Ephesus, the professing Christians. If you stop to think about it, this is a very stern warning. If they were dead, that means that they had no real faith, that they did not have or maybe were not waking in the light of Christ.

He continues to tell them to walk circumspectly in other words taking special care how they walked, or in the Christian sense, how they lived their lives. He tells them to redeem or make good the times, because the days they lived in were evil.

Overly concerned with secondary doctrines; (end times, blessing Israel, manifestation of gifts, etc.) or false doctrines; (like prosperity or comfort of the believer). These things tend to put us to sleep to the light of Christ.

We may not even be concerned with "redeeming" the time that

we have; in other words, making the most of the time we have, to buy back the time (from the world, the flesh, an the devil). Making the most of the time is to make our times spent more Christ centered, putting those around us in the center of His will, as best as we can. Or changing our habits so that we are more about His business and less about ours.

We do this because we, like the Ephesians, live in evil days, and these days can be redeemed into what the Lord desires, not what the devil does. Every day we have the power within us to redeem the day, no matter what evil is around us.

Ephesians 5:8 For you were once darkness, but now you are light in the Lord. Walk as children of light

Ephesians 5:17 is the clincher: it says that to understand the will of the Lord is wisdom. It makes us wise instead of foolish.

So, what is His will is for us, except to know Him and to obey Him. Those are the things I most always write about, being a disciple of Jesus, following His light and taking that light to the world.

Psalm 89:15 Blessed are the people who know the joyful sound! They walk, O LORD, in the light of Your countenance.

Be Blessed in Him Today
Philippine Bible Ministry

DEATH WHICH LEADS TO LIFE

John 12:24 Most assuredly, I say to you, unless a grain of wheat falls into the ground and dies, it remains alone; but if it dies, it produces much grain.

This passage explains how a believer grows and changes. How we are to become life giving people; that life that we give is Him. The offer of Him living in others.

It is actually the progression of life for all believers who trust in Him.

I often think of Moses in conjunction with the grain of wheat verse.

Moses, who was raised as a Prince of Egypt; he was chosen to lead God's people out of bondage and into the promised land. He had such an intimate face to face relationship with God that his face shone with the glory of the Lord after his conversations

Exodus 24:29 Now it was so, when Moses came down from Mount Sinai (and the two tablets of the Testimony were in Moses' hand when he came down from the mountain), that Moses did not know that the skin of his face shone while he talked with Him.

He of course did not start out as one that had this amazing life giving face to face relationship with the Lord.

It was a very fleshly and proud Moses who thought he could save the Jews by killing one of their overseers to protect a few that were being beaten.

Imagine that guy, thinking he could defy Pharaoh by killing one of his stewards. Thinking that the Jews would accept him, just like that.

Do not believe the Hollywood version, where Moses did not even know he was a Jew. His birth mother was chosen to be his nurse maid; that meant that she would have nursed him and cared for him for at least the first 5 years of his life (if not more), probably she taught him about his true heritage when he was very young, I believe he knew he was a Jew, and he believed that being a Prince of Egypt they would embrace him as their leader.

Moses soon found out that not only did Pharaoh seek to take his life because he dared to kill one of his trusted overseers.; but that the Jews likewise would not have him and did not trust him.

Moses ran away into the wilderness; stripped of all he had. Two families; and all of the trimmings of being a rich young ruler. A form of death, you might say.

Unless that seed of wheat dies it remains lifeless.

Moses 40 years in the wilderness, tending sheep and raising a family; sort of like that time in the soil when new life begins to sprout. Then one day the Lord spoke to Him out of that burning bush. Like one day that sprout broke up from the soil. Just like that seed eventually grew into a large stalk of wheat which contains much life. Moses eventually grew into that man that led millions out of bondage, and made these people (at least the ones that finally made it into the promised land) into a great nation of God. Thereby producing great life because he experienced a personal death like experience.

So it is with us, if we are willing to bend to His will, He will put our flesh to death in some way, then; in time, we shall also produce much Lord's life in those around us

Be Blessed in Him Today
Philippine Bible Ministry

TURN OR BURN

Repentance::

Hebrew: nâcham, pronounced na-cham; meaning *to be sorry*

Greek: metanoeō Pronunciation: met-an-o-eh'-o: meaning: <u>to change one mind for the better, to turn around</u>

.

When you put these two words together in the Hebrew and the Greek you get the true sense of the word "repent": To be sorry, change ones mind about something, and turn around or turn away from that thing.

You need to be sorry for your sins. It is not just about accepting Jesus, the reason we need Him is our sins. Jesus died for our sins, you must first be sorry for your sins. So what about the word sin?

Sin

Hebrew: chaṭṭâ'âh pronounced khat-taw-aw'; meaning <u>an offense that has a penalty</u>Greek: hamartia Pronunciation: ham-ar-tee'-ah, meaning <u>to miss the mark</u>

Another Greek word translated sin skandalizō Pronunciation: skan-dal-id'-zo. Which means <u>to cause one to stumble</u>

So putting all that together to sin is :

<u>not do things the right way which offends someone (God) causing others to stumble,</u>

So when we repent we change our minds and turn from our sins, of not doing things the right way, which of course is God's way.

This means that when we are saved we are expected to repent from the sin in our lives, to turn from it. To do things God's way. Repentance does not save you, but it is the proof that you are saved

Luke 5:32 32 I have not come to call the righteous, but sinners, to repentance." Jesus called sinners to repentance, not just a profession of faith, but an active faith.

Luke 24:46 Then He said to them, "Thus it is written, and thus it was necessary for the Christ to suffer and to rise from the dead the third day, 47 and that repentance and remission of sins should be preached in His name to all nations, beginning at Jerusalem. Once saved, repentance from and remission of sin are the marks of salvation

When the apostles preached in Acts, they called people to repent of their sins in order to be forgiven (See **Acts 2:38, 3:19, 8:32, 17:30, 20:21, 26:20**). It is the visible evidence of the work of the Holy Spirit in our lives.

The apostle Paul makes it clear that those whose lives are characterized by sin "will not inherit the kingdom of God" (**1 Cor. 6:9-10; see also Rom. 8:12-13, Gal. 5:21, Eph. 5:5**)

None of this means that we will be perfectly sinless, it just means that we will walk away from our sins, and when we do stumble, it will be an occasional occurrence, not a habitual one;not as it was before we knew Him and called Him Lord

Be Blessed in Him Today
Philippine Bible Ministry

EVERYBODY WANTS TO GO TO HEAVEN, BUT NOBODY WANTS TO DIE

Romans 8:36 36 As it is written: "For Your sake we are killed all day long; We are accounted as sheep for the slaughter.

If you have been around church for any amount of time, you may have heard a pastor say something like, 'it is easier to die for Christ than to live for Him". Meaning that it is probably easier to make a stance and get killed for you belief, than it is to live day by day for Him.

The daily grind can lead to a steady slow decay of ones walk with Jesus.

But as I was listening to an old sermon from AW Tozer this morning, One of my favorite Old Time Master. He was speaking about dying for Christ in a different way

.

Here is the example: Two preachers are getting up there in age, maybe 70 something, both are told by their doctors that they need to retire and remove themselves from stressful situations, or else they will die soon. One man quits his ministry job; sells his home and moves to Florida to retire and rest. He sits around for many years, just sitting around and resting.

The other man, he keeps his ministry position, in fact since he knows that he may not have much time left on this earth; he works twice as hard to bring more souls with him to heaven. He does not live too many years more. He is a happy man, especially when he meets his Lord. He hears

:Matthew 25:23 His lord said to him, 'Well done, good and faithful servant; you have been faithful over a few things, I will make you ruler over many things. Enter into the joy of your lord.'.

Tozer speaks of changing on to life, like the last leaf to drop from a tree, how it is kind of a limp response to life, and most importantly to the Lord. When the time is ripe go ahead and die for Him, no regrets.

I was particularly impacted by this thought myself, as a man that is approaching his 70's. I feel that much like that second man; I want to go out in a blaze of glory, right smack dab in the middle of His will.:

Galatians 2:20 I have been crucified with Christ; it is no longer I who live, but Christ lives in me; and the life which I now live in the flesh I live by faith in the Son of God, who loved me and gave Himself for me.

I know my wife would argue that point, but she does understand my heart and how much I want to be used of God. Nothing is more important to me. And remarkably I find that the older I get, the bolder I get. We wait; and when the right time comes, we have Gods' power lifting us to His work, no matter our age:

Isaiah 40:31: But they that wait upon the LORD shall renew their strength; they shall mount up with wings as eagles; they shall run, and not be weary; and they shall walk, and not faint.

Be Blessed in Him Today
Philippine Bible Ministry

DISCIPLES ARE TEACHABLE.

Keep me humble and small
in my own eyes

Thanks to Fenelon and Job this morning for reminding me that I need to be careful in my thirst for all things Theological, my idea is to learn about most all of the doctrines in the Church, so that I know exactly what to focus on in a ministry that is to be focused on essentials. It seems to me that I cannot do this unless I know something of these doctrines.

As I have discovered that many of the doctrines that I had been taught since 1993 have not been very sound biblically, have been huge distractions to the mandates of Jesus. It has been difficult. To see that so many of the churches out there are kind of out there. Even if you could show them in the Bible where what they have been saying for years has been off, they would not listen.

Would I listen? And do I listen?

I pray and hope that I will always listen, not to trust in church movements or in great pastor/teachers. But always to look to the Bible.

Here is an example right now. If you read these posts you will know that I hold the Puritans in high esteem. So it happened this week that I ran into an obstacle in that view. It is their assertion that the doctrine of Free Will, is not only incorrect; but that it is actually blasphemous.

More on that latter, as I am in process of investigation. This goes against what I believe, I am of the belief that both Predestination and Free Will are somehow correct. But when I run into this cloud of witnesses, all of these Bible teachers of old that have a strong opinion; like Charles Spurgeon, for example. I cannot just throw them out, I need to at least respect their studies enough to give them a good hearing.

It reminds me of the many doctrines that I have discovered (though they may be thousands of years old) that have caused me to change my views.

And that I believe that many if not most of the Christians that I know personally will think I am crazy to walk away from the stuff we have been taught.

But we must be humble enough to give these folks an honest listen.

Look at Eschatology for example. What do we do? We read books that believe what we believe and strengthen those beliefs. But do we ever consider looking at the writings of others? Not usually' this begs the question: Are you married to your pet doctrines or are you married to the Lord?

Most of the things that I am talking about are not even essential for your Salvation, not even essential for your Sanctification. But we think on them, we spend out time and money on them, we spend more time on some of these doctrines, than we do in following Him. I mean by that, we pretend that these doctrines has something to do with His will, when in fact they have more to do with our own will

Be Blessed in Him Today
Philippine Bible Ministry

WHO DO YOU SEE
IN YOUR SELFIES?

1 Corinthians 13:10 For now we see in a mirror, dimly, but then face to face. Now I know in part, but then I shall know just as I also am known.

We do not truly see ourselves in this life. We see dimly, in fact we see ourselves through a darkness that is due to sin.
The world the flesh and the devil. All of these things cloud our view of ourselves. In fact we see ourselves as way too important. That is why selfies are so popular. In the words of Terrell Owens, we "Love me some me"

In this world we love our youth, and you see a lot of selfies that prove that. Your beauty will fade your body will decay we are like a cut rose, so beautiful today, but in a few days, it begins to look bad, soon shriveling up and wilting to nothing. Thus, it is with our flesh. Our lives are but a vapor in the sands of eternity. This physical life of the flesh is not the part of us that has value. No, it is our spirit. And to see our spiritual self, for the Christian, we need to see that we are to become a new creation. And we can only see that self though the mirror of the Bible.

The Bible will tell us that we were born in sin. That without the Lords intervention and our acceptance of that, we would never be anything more than a short-lived flower, the rest is all decay and death.

But in Him. We are becoming new, we need to take that seriously, to live our life in Him means to grasp that abundant life He promises. It means to live your life for Him

Near the end of one's life you will never hear a Christian say these things:
"I regret not working more"
"I regret praying too much"
"I regret giving too much to the Lords work"

But you may hear them say this:
 "I regret not giving more of my life to Christ"

Do not be the one that can honestly say that at the end of your life.

I think that the "Beema Seat of Christ", or some would call it "The Judgement Seat of Christ"
(1 Cor. 3:10-14) does not get enough respect these days. Someday the Christian's life will be judged, not for Salvation, that is settled, but how did you spend your life, the life that He gave you, and the life that He died on the cross for. How did you use that gift of life that He gave you?

How every many days you have left on earth, spend them well.

By His grace we Christians can come to the throne of God, but we must be humble and contrite when we come. We can only come when we are summoned, of course because of the cross, we are always called to come to Him. But you must know that Jesus is so powerful, it is not a light thing to be before the King of the Universe.

CS Lewis once said of the Lord in The Lion, the Witch, and The Wardrobe "He is not a tame lion and He is not safe, but He is good"

Come to Him now, with a humble and contrite heart, and ask Him what He would have you do with your short life on earth. Then do it.

Our lives should not look like the lives of the world around us. In our selfie's others should see the image of Jesus Christ

We will never say at the end of our lives that we regret giving too much of our lives to Jesus Christ
Be Blessed in Him Today   Philippine Bible Ministry

WE KNOW THAT JESUS TOLD US TO DO <u>ONLY A FEW THINGS</u>,

*maybe these few things are what
we should in fact focus on?*

1. Go and make disciples of the nations, (baptizing them in His name)
2. Be baptized
3. Take communion
4. Love God and Love one another
5. Pray

In focusing on lesser things, we may not actually be in His will. Jesus manifested Himself to the world for the purpose of destroying the works of Satan. The essential doctrines do that. The non-essentials do not do that.

End-Times Theology example of a non-essential doctrine; the outcome of all End Times doctrines is exactly the same: Be Ready!! Here is the little trick that you do not need to study books on end times or go to seminars or follow pastors that seem to be stuck in their version of End Times. All you need do is walk in Him daily. I hereby pronounce you ready if you are His dis-

NOTIONS ON THE CHRISTIAN LIFE:

ciple...........YOUR WELCOME.

The Check yourself if you are His. Do you spend time at least praying for the conversion of this world? Do you spend your time and $$$$ on that? Your heart and mind?

Let us all, especially me, be open to different views on these non-essentials. I pray that we can and will be open to His will in our lives.

BeBlessedinHimToday   Philippine Bible Ministry

WHAT IS A DISCIPLE OF JESUS CHRIST?

One of the most, if not the most, important command of our Lord Jesus is to:
"Go and make disciples of the nations" Matthew 28:19

That means the goal is for all nations, in other words, all people groups, to become disciples of the Lord. Which means that the goal is for all to be disciples of Christ.

That means that we need to understand two things here.

1. What exactly does disciple mean?

2. What things should a disciple learn, know, or follow?

In the original language it says to go and teach, not to make disciples. But when we look up the word teach (I use the Textus Receptus Bibles website).

The word is mathēteuō

Thayer's Lexicon of Greek:

1. to be a disciple of one; a. to follow his precepts and instructions

2. to make a disciple; a. to teach, instruct

The Strong's definition is likewise:

intransitively to become a pupil; transitively to disciple

It pretty much means what we think it means, to make them students of the Lord Jesus. To learn about Him and then to follow Him. To know Gods word so that we can then follow Him.

Here is what it does NOT mean: To teach ones denominational doctrines, or to make a follower of a specific church.

Is that an important distinction?

Well, I'm not so sure. It might be fine; most denominations do

NOTIONS ON THE CHRISTIAN LIFE:

have the basics correct. You know saved by faith in Christ, not be works, and "Jesus is God and Man' and that God is "One God in three distinct persons"

Some of these side issues though; they produce more division in the body, which is probable NOT what Jesus had in mind when He said. Go and make disciples.
I recently sought advice from a pastor that has been doing missionary work since the 80's. He was great and that hour I spent with him was well invested,
He said something to me that has strengthened my belief that God does not want me to establish Churches per se in the Philippines, but to make these "disciples"

He said that he helped to establish a bible college in the Philippines, and that he had some mixed feelings, some regrets perhaps, that when young Pastors to be showed up they were converted to that denomination. He thought that was not exactly right. After all why would you take the best and brightest from other denominations and "convert" them. Is it not better to stick to the basics?
So, the Basics for discipleship, I think are pretty simple.
· Faith in Christ, and
· Trust as the disciple moves out in Him,
· Spreading of the simple faith
· Acceptance of different beliefs on the non-essentials
That is why we will be teaching the straight word of God. The focus will be on
· Bible
· Prayer
· Salvation by faith in Him
· Baptism into the Body of Christ (not into a denomination)
· Spreading of disciples throughout Philippines (and maybe even the USA)
· Strong and Rigid on the essentials
· Grace for the non-essentials
I hope that makes sense to you

We need to know the essentials so that we can then Obey Jesus Christ, because that is what a disciple would do,
Looks like I need a post to review, what is essential and what is not, at least as far as I understand it
Be blessed in Him as you learn to be His (not anyone else's) disciple

BeBlessedinHimToday   Philippine Bible Ministry

JUMP IN THE DEEP
WITH JESUS

In the book of Ezekiel (chapter 47) the prophet is shown a future temple out of which water flows. The further that one goes out into this river the deeper it becomes

Ezekiel 47: 3 And when the man who had the line in his hand went forth eastward, he measured a thousand cubits, and he brought me through the waters; the waters were to the ankles. 4 Again he measured a thousand and brought me through the waters; the waters were to the knees. Again, he measured a thousand, and brought me through; the waters were to the loins.5 Afterward he measured a thousand, and it was a river that I could not pass over; for the waters had risen, waters to swim in, a river that could not be passed over.

This river from Gods temple has usually been interpreted by Christian to mean the Church or Salvation. It could also be the work of the Holy Spirit which is also the Church The reason is that as the river flows out it brings life wherever it goes:

[6] He said to me, "Son of man, have you seen *this*?" Then he brought me and returned me to the bank of the river.[7] When I returned, there, along the bank of the river, *were* very many trees on one side and the other. [8] Then he said to me: "This water flows toward the eastern region, goes down into the valley, and enters the sea. *When it* reaches the sea, *its* waters are healed. [9] And it shall be *that* every living thing that moves, wherever the rivers go, will live. There will be a very great multitude of fish, because

these waters go there; for they will be healed, and everything will live wherever the river goes

The healing which flows from the Holy Spirit to the world is by way of the Church of Christ.

If the river is the work of the Holy Spirit or the Church, than it makes sense that it is the body of Christ, the works done as the believer walks in Him. That the Lord uses us to bring salvation to this world. Also, to bring sanctification or holiness to the world.

So, the beginnings are shallow water, only to the ankles for 1,000 cubits. Sounds like the Church in the West today. Wide but shallow, with no power, and I think even more significantly; no trust in Him. The shallows require no faith as anyone can stand in ankle deep water, it requires no effort. No faith, it costs us nothing. But it feels real cool and comfortable.

But Christ has asked us to take up our cross. To share in His sufferings, to jump into the deep end. The place where we cannot touch and we would be tossed about by the water. Well, that water is the Holy Spirit.

You see, the Holy Spirit power and life quires much faith, and it costs us our sure footing in this world. It is a trade, the sure footing of the things of this world, versus the trust to jump into His water, and to give up our safe life.

Do you think you could ever do that?

Just give up some of your comfy ways and trust Him with the outcome. Fully trusting.

Do you think He would make your new life the best life you could ever have?

That the blessings would come in such abundance Not material blessings, those are temporary and weak, No the true blessing of Himself.

Jump in today.

BeBlessedinHimToday
ippine Bible Ministry

Phil-

WHAT DO WE GIVE THE LORD?

Jesus gave His life for us on the cross
He came to earth made himself into a servant and suffered for us
What do we give Him in return?
Not for our salvation, that is settled at the cross. No this is about our life as a believer. What is our response to His gift? Besides gratitude, love, etc.?
Our sins?

The Lord doesn't want your nasty old sins. He wants you. He takes our sins and forgives us. But is that all we give Him? Is that all there is to it? No He wants you, all of you Sacrificed on the altar

Romans 12:1 I beseech you therefore, brethren, by the mercies of God, that you present your bodies a living sacrifice, holy, acceptable to God, which is your reasonable service.

Your body here is your flesh, your physical and emotional life. pretty much everything of you that is not of Him. And when God pours out His Fire. It is then that we are burnt on that altar. It's the sacrifice that is burnt up. Not the altar
John the Baptist spoke of Jesus and the coming baptism by fire when he said in

Matthew 3:11 11 I indeed baptize you with water unto repent-

ance, but He who is coming after me is mightier than I, whose sandals I am not worthy to carry. He will baptize you with the Holy Spirit and fire.

Your rights, your comforts, your desires. All of it burned up there by and for Him
Not that we all need to give all of our possessions to Him, but we all should be WILLING to do what Jesus asked the Rich Young Ruler to do

Luke 18:22
So, when Jesus heard these things, He said to him, "You still lack one thing. Sell all that you have and distribute to the poor, and you will have treasure in heaven; and come, follow Me."

Then what is left? Well, what is left is what He gives us.
A new heart.
A soft heart

Ezekiel 11:10 Then I will give them one heart, and I will put a new spirit within them, and take the stony heart out of their flesh, and give them a heart of flesh,

Then that new soft heart will be in His will, and then He will give us the right desires, His desires:

Psalm 37:4 Delight yourself also in the Lord, And He shall give you the desires of your heart.

It takes a lot to get us to that Abraham place.

By faith Abraham, when he was tested, offered up Isaac, and he who had received the promises offered up his only begotten son,
Offered that son that he waited until he was 100 years old.
In total surrender, he offered up all the promise that God had made to him.
That place of total surrender to sacrifice the one you love. which in the truth of it is yourself, No one loves others as much as they love themselves?

The Lord did not take Isaac from Abraham, but the man's faith was complete in this act.

The Lord will take your flesh and then your faith will also be complete

This is one way that God tests your faith

to see if and when you are ready to lay it all out, to put your family, spouse, children, everything on that altar than comes the blessing:

James 1:3-4

3 knowing that the testing of your faith produces [a]patience. 4 But let patience have its perfect work, that you may be perfect and complete, lacking nothing

This is all part of that second blessing you may have heard about, the Sanctification available to those that are saved.

BeBlessedinHimToday   Philippine Bible Ministry

WHAT IS A DISCIPLE OF JESUS CHRIST?

One of the most, if not the most, important command of our Lord Jesus is to **"Go and make disciples of the nations"**

That means the goal is for all nations, in other words, all people groups, to become disciples of the Lord. Which means that the goal is for all to be disciples of Christ.
That means that we need to understand two things here.

1. What exactly does disciple mean?
2. What things should a disciple learn, know, or follow?

In the original language it says to go and teach, not to make disciples. But when we look up the word teach (I use the Textus Receptus Bibles website).

The word is *mathēteuō:*

Thayer's Lexicon of Greek
1. to be a disciple of one; a. to follow his precepts and instructions
2. to make a disciple; a. to teach, instruct

The Strong's definition is likewise:
to become a pupil; to disciple that is enrolled under a scholar

It pretty much means what we think it means, to make them students of the Lord Jesus. To learn about Him and then to follow Him. To know Gods word so that we can then follow Him.
Here is what it does NOT mean: To teach your own denomin-

ational doctrines, or to make a follower of a specific church, or even a follower of you or anyone besides Jesus Himself.

Is that an important distinction?
I recently sought advice from a pastor that has been doing missionary work in the Philippines since the 80's. He was great and that hour I spent with him was well invested.
He said something to me that has strengthened my belief that God does not want me to establish Churches per se in the Philippines, but to make these "disciples"

He said that he helped to establish a bible college in the Philippines, and that he had some regrets; perhaps, when young Pastors to be showed up they were converted to that denomination. He thought that was not right. After all, why would you take the best and brightest from other denominations and "convert" them? Is it not better to stick to the basics amnd let each on follow Christ instead of a denomination?

The Basics for discipleship, I think are pretty simple:
· Faith in Christ, and
· Trust as the disciple moves out in Him,
· Spreading of the simple faith
· Acceptance of different beliefs on the non-essentials

That is why we will be teaching the straight word of God. The focus will be on
· Bible
· Prayer
· Salvation by faith in Him
· Baptism into the Body of Christ (not into a denomination)
· Spreading of disciples throughout Philippines (and maybe even the USA)
· Strong and Rigid on the essentials
· Grace for the non-essentials
I hope that makes sense to you

We need to know the essentials so that we can then Obey Jesus

Christ, because that is what a disciple would do.

Be blessed as you learn to be His (not anyone else's) disciple

Be Blessed in Him Today
Philippine Bible Ministry

WHAT IS SANCTIFICATION?

Sanctification means to be set apart for a purpose. God has a special purpose for all of His children.

All who believe in Him become His children of faith, some call it the Church, the Body of Christ, or True Believers. Nowadays we have a kind of milk toast definition as people of faith; that doesn't really cut it for me because it does not define the faith, a person that believes in themselves, or the earth, or the dollar, or their political party, all of these can be persons of faith.

Sanctification is what is supposed to follow Salvation. It is one of the tests of whether or not your church body is solid or wispy. So many Christian Churches seek salvation and then keep seeking it and then keep telling everyone that they are still saved and how much God loves them and accepts whatever they do, no change of heart needed.

But once you are truly saved, that is once there is evidence of your salvation by a change in your heart, your mind, your lifestyle, once you are truly His. When that happens you will find a thirst and a hunger for the things of God, and the things that once brought you such pleasure, well many of these things will no longer attract you. So at that point, when you are born again, at that point, you no longer just want some kind of feeling or experience at Church, at that point you want to meet God at Church. And at that point you want to follow, to serve, to know Him, and yes even to obey Him

So the Bible tells us that before the foundations, before God

formed the earth, He knew you
(Jeremiah 1), He has a plan for you.

We know that in all things God works for good with those who love him, those whom he has called according to his purpose. **(Romans 8:28)**

To be part of His purpose. At some point you need to let go of your own goals and seek His goals. At that point the blessing will come, for that is the abundant life He has for you. When it says that He will give you the desires of your heart, don't be mistaken, that does not mean He will give you everything you want. <u>It means that you will want the things that He wants</u>. His desires will be yours, at that point your prayers will be answered because they will be in Jesus name (or His will)

1 Cor 13:11 When I was a child, I spoke as a child, I understood as a child, I thought as a child; but when I became a man, I put away childish things.

Sanctification is a growing up type of Christianity, that's why it's not too popular in the modern world or the modern church for that matter. The modern world is more concerned with childish demands and such than it is with growing up.

GROWING UP IN, BY, AND FOR HIM....

I'LL TAKE THAT AS A GOOD DEFINITION OF SANCTIFICATION

I know that it sounds strange, I have many Christian peers that accuse me of being too strong in this. Is it possible to be too strong in the Lord of Creation? I think not. But you know that when those in church do not like certain things in the Bible they just call it legalism.

My prayer is that someone reading this will be convicted enough to seek Him today and ask Him if you should pursue sanctification.

It may be lonely to follow God in this way.

"The loneliness of the Christian results from his walk with God in an ungodly world, a walk that must often take him away from the fellowship of good Christians as well as from that of the unregenerate world.

His God-given instincts cry out for companionship with others of his kind, others who can understand his longings, his aspirations, his absorption in the love of Christ; and because within his circle of friends there are so few who share his inner experiences he is often forced to walk alone. The unsatisfied longings of the prophets for human understanding caused them to cry out in their complaint, and even our Lord Himself suffered in the same way."
Oswald Chambers

Be Blessed in Him Today
Philippine Bible Ministry

TRUST IN HIM

If you honestly believe that the Lord is calling you to do something, then ask for confirmation, then step out in it. Then you trust Him to do it. Do not run around asking others to give you advice about how to do it, or even asking for help. If you know God wants you to do it, and it has been confirmed by circumstances or by others (without asking) then all you need to do is tell others what you are going to do.

If what you are called to do takes provision of which you have none, then turst that God will provide for His work. You do not need to call every Christian that you know to ask for money. That is not trusting in Him. If they find out about what you are doing and offer you something, then that is different. But trust Him.

George Mueller was a special Christian man that lived in the 19th century. When converted George and a good friend heard the story of a missionary couple that sold everything and went on the mission field, trusting God to supply their every need. At that point he made a pact with his friend that they would live that way for the rest of their lives. Never asking a penny from anyone, and totally relying on God to supply their needs. I would tell you that his needs were met, but it went much deeper than that. George Muller build several homes for street orphans and saved thousands from lives of destitute poverty. He had received Over 117 Million dollars! And He never asked for one donation. He trusted God and the donations came in.

What a breath of fresh air, I must admit that it goes against our very nature not to run a donation campaign, but God is in control; if we believe that, then He will provide for His ministries. If He does not provide, then it is probably not from Him. That does not mean it will not be difficult and that there will not be dark days and nights when waiting for His provision. But wait on Him and He will prove trustworthy.

How many ministries do that today? And why not? I support a few ministries myself, and they often ask for help, and it is fine to do that. But how glorious would it be, to just trust in Him.

Taylor Hudson the great missionary to China lived such a life. He and his wife would be without medicine or food for the people, and just at the right time a check would arrive (sometimes from George Mueller) which would supply their needs. They would then thank God for not giving them this gift ahead of time, so that they could know the blessing of the God that supplies right on time.

There are lots of similar stories. God is good and supplies the needs of His people. (but not always their wants)Today we do not even think of such things, why who in their right minds would sell all they have and follow Him. Maybe, just Maybe the ones that will receive the biggest blessings.

Try some baby steps in this then see what He will do.

BeBlessedinHimToday   Philippine Bible Ministry

GET ALONE WITH GOD

Jesus certainly spent many hours alone in prayer with the Father **"He went up on a mountainside by Himself to pray. When evening came, He was there alone." (Matthew 14:23)**

The following is a true story from Leonard Ravenhill:

There was a black man in South Africa, his name was Dumas. He went into a Baptist church one night and the Lord came upon him and he got wonderfully saved. And when he got to the door the preacher said, "Well nice to see you. Hope you come again." He said, "Yes." "Anything I can do for you?" And he, 'said yes, yes, yes sir there is." He said "What?" He said "Give me a church. "What did you say?" He said, "Give me a church. I've been looking all my life for the thing I found there at that altar." And he said "Listen, I'm a new man. My burden's gone! I felt the fetters break! I felt the burden go from off my back! I felt something surging and making me pure and wonderful! I want to tell everybody! Give me a church to preach."

"Oh well... have you had much formal education?" 'No.' "Have you been to bible school?" 'No.' Well that was an advantage if he'd only known. And he hadn't been to bible school, and so finally the preacher said, "You just keep coming." "But man," he said "this is wonderful. I'd heard it preached about being a new creation, but it happened in my life and I'm a new creature; old things have passed away. You know, I don't have a desire; I don't have appetite. Everything's new! I want God I want God I want God!!

He came back a month later. The preacher was preaching and thinking "Now who's that fellow there? Yes, I know, I know, yea,

yea, yea I know who he is, I think I know who he is. And going out he said, "Hi brother how are you?" he said "Fine." He said "I'd like to ask you a question." and he said "Go ahead" the preacher said. He said "Would you give me a church?" "Yes I thought you were the fellow, only been in church twice and you ask for a church each time you come. Do you think I have a pocket full of them or something, and here's one for you and one for...?

He said "Sir your right I haven't been here for a month. When you told me at the door you'd see me again," He said "Sir I walked up that road outside of the city, I found a forest, I went in the forest I found a path, I found a stream, I found a cave there, and I put a mark on the wall and I stayed there 21 days and 21 night with my Bible." And he said "Lord you and I just the two of us, we're going to have it out. I was not going to leave that place until I had assurance, either 'I called you to minister?' or did I go out and say 'you will never get me to preach?' It's one of the two." He said "I ate no bread, I talked with nobody, I washed my face in the stream, and right in the middle of that 21 days the Holy Ghost came upon me. And the Spirit said, 'I've called you to preach. And when you lay hands on the sick, the sick will recover. Go ahead.' Are you going to give me a church?"

"Well, we do have an elder's meeting on Wednesday night." If you could come back on Sunday." And the elders discussed it and said, "You know, he's a bit of a freak, you're not going to get rid of him. Now we do have a little tin church out on the other side of town, you know a shack, why not give it to him? it's only got 5 members. And you know, he's ignorant and rude, and his grammar isn't good, and he couldn't deal with a text very well, he couldn't... truth is, all he'd do is ill treat it.

And the people wouldn't want to go hear him after a few days, a few weeks, and they will close it down and say, 'You see, you weren't called.'"

But what happened? That little church grew and grew and before long they moved to a bigger and better church. And Dumas became one of the greatest preachers that South Africa has ever seen.

The man had found out the secret, it is to get alone with God. You know for the next 17 years, it was said, that he would go back to that cave and spend another 21 days alone with God each year. How much time will you spend alone with Him?

BeBlessedinHimToday   Philippine Bible Ministry

DENY YOURSELF

"If anyone desires to come after Me, let him deny himself..." (Luke 9:23).

The Lord never forces anyone to obey Him. Sanctification can only happen if you are willing to surrender to Him. It is an action of the heart, mind and soul.

This type of dedication is hard to find in our modern Church. Mostly we see lots of emotional responses the Lord, and many proclaim that they love Him because that is so easy to feel. I feel love for the Lord every day, most of the day. It is second nature to a believer. And the emotions of it are easy to stir up with nice sweet music and nice sweet preaching. Nothing wrong with it.

However, where does it leave us. Michael W Smith has a line from his song "Give it away": "The road to good intentions doesn't lead you anywhere, cause love isn't love till you give it away"

This is not about salvation; this is about being of value to the God who gave you that life of yours. It's about an active faith. Oh and maybe it is a bit about salvation, because without works faith is dead. **(James 2)**

He is not talking about rules to follow; He is talking about following Him.

Do you desire Him or just His blessings?

Do you know Him, or just know about Him?

Would you dare pray that He would break your heart with the things that break His heart? And if He does that are you prepared to do anything, go anywhere, do anything that He might ask of you?

Pray that you may become one with the Spirit as you lean into

Him

Pray that you would be obedient to this Lord who gave it all for you.

Pray that you would fulfill your destiny in Him.

Pray that the Love of God will flow through you today.

Be Blessed in Him

Philippine Bible Ministry

CUP OF SUFFERING

I now rejoice in my sufferings for you, and fill up in my flesh what is lacking in the afflictions of Christ, for the sake of His body, which is the church Colossians 1:24

Jesus promised the Holy Spirit would come to empower the believers and lead them in all things
But why didn't He give them the Spirit right then?
Jesus told them that He must suffer and they also would sorrow.

John 16:20
20 Most assuredly, I say to you that you will weep and lament, but the world will rejoice; and you will be sorrowful, but your sorrow will be turned into joy.

There would have been no outpouring of the Holy Spirit, without Gethsemane. In the garden Jesus surrendered to the cross. He drank the cup of suffering.

I have news for you, that you probably will not hear in most pulpits today. He also asks you if you will share in this cup of suffering. That is, if you want to be His disciple.

You do want to be His disciple, don't you?

Mark 10:38 But Jesus said to them, "You do not know what you ask. Are you able to drink the cup that I drink, and be baptized with the baptism that I am baptized with?"39 They said to Him, "We are able." So Jesus said to them, "You will indeed drink the cup that I drink, and with the baptism I am baptized with you will be baptized

They wanted the blessings of God, not realizing there is a price to pay, not for salvation, do not be confused. But there is a price to pay to be His disciple, the second blessing it is called: Sanctification. It starts with your surrender to Him. Not just some emotional response to a worship song or even to a sermon. No it is a personal thing. It will be made real to you, when the fire starts. Look at the disciples of Christ in the bible
:

Paul

, 2 Corinthians 11:

4 From the Jews five times I received forty stripes minus one. 25 Three times I was beaten with rods; once I was stoned; three times I was shipwrecked; a night and a day I have been in the deep; 26 in journeys often, in perils of waters, in perils of robbers, in perils of my own countrymen, in perils of the Gentiles, in perils in the city, in perils in the wilderness, in perils in the sea, in perils among false brethren; 27 in weariness and toil, in sleeplessness often, in hunger and thirst, in fasting often, in cold and nakedness—

The other apostles were all martyred (except for John). Jesus told Peter that he would need to suffer, due to His obedience to the Lord, he was crucified (according to tradition, upside down and next to his wife.

Taylor Hudson who founded the inland China Missions lost his child and his wife, in fact many missionaries lost family and some lost their lives early in their pursuit of the calling that God gave them. Jim Elliot, William Cary, Amy Carmichael, etc.

David Brainerd was the first missionary to the Native Americans in the 1700's' he literally gave his life in prayer and travail in the elements to serve the lord, he would pray all night in the wilderness waking in the snow; he passed at the age of 29. Jonathan Edwards daughter would risk her life to minister to him on his death bed, she became ill and herself passed away from the same consumption that killed him.

Why would you think that the world would treat you better, or why would you think that you would not suffer as our Lord suffered. In this day of comfort and prosperity, no one wants to hear the truth.

But the good news is that if you stay in Him and push through; He will bless you beyond measure. And your treasure will be great in heaven.

Mark 10:29
So, Jesus answered and said, "Assuredly, I say to you, there is no one who has left house or brothers or sisters or father or mother [c]or wife or children or lands, for My sake and the gospel's, 30 who shall not receive a hundredfold now in this time—houses and brothers and sisters and mothers and children and lands, with persecutions—and in the age to come, eternal life. 31 But many who are first will be last, and the last first."

Note the words in the middle: WITH PERSECUTIONS. True Christianity is not for cowards.

If you are ready to put on your grown-up clothes; then, follow Him.

1 Corinthians 13:11 When I was a child, I spoke as a child, I understood as a child, I thought as a child; but when I became a man, I put away childish things.

Not what you may want to hear, but maybe what you need to hear, that is if you want to see Gods Revival in this world, or at least to follow Him

BeBlessedinHimToday   Philippine Bible Ministry

WHAT IF GOD WANTS YOU FOR SOMETHING?

Recently read an article about poll numbers for social issues amongst Americans. You know, gay marriage, marijuana use, church attendance, professed Christians.

Wasn't surprised by any of it. It just confirmed what I have come to believe. That the modern church is not alive. Even with all the fancy, concert like, worship and the "dynamic" mega churches with there "amazing" teachings. Seem to fall short

Why is this? I know that many feel really good after going to church. If they hear a good message, they will tell each other how great that was. And yet, come Monday there is virtually no change in their lives.

Maybe, just maybe, there is a better way to do this?

If you have been churched for 10,20, or even 30 years and do not find yourself thirsting or longing for a stronger closer walk with Him. Then it might be time

What if?.................................

God wanted all His children. His followers, His Church to have a faith that produced active Christianity?

What if He wanted all of us to actively live FOR HIM?

To put aside our worldly ways and pursue those works that He has prepared for us?

To be part of fellowships small enough where each one can learn how to use the gifts God gave them, not just a teacher and a bunch of feeding sheep, but a body of faith filled with believers operating in those gifts?

To be led by each other in true And committed fellowship. Not just coffee and donuts and light chit chat after service. But to share our lives. Our hopes and our struggles. Our walks with each other?

What if God were to raise up these new types of fellowships in your town?

Would you be able to follow this new/old way?

Or would you just stay in your comfortable pews and keep doing this church thing you have always done

◆◆◆◆◆◆◆◆◆◆◆◆◆◆◆◆◆◆◆◆◆◆◆◆◆

It's happening here and now.

My favorite new V show is an amazing multi season view of Christ's ministry called _The Chosen_

Simon is upset that Jesus brings in tax collectors and visits Samaria to start His ministry.

"It's different ". Simon says

"Get used to different "Jesus tell him

BeBlessedinHimToday   Philippine Bible Ministry

LIFE IS A PART TIME JOB

I have been saying this since before I was a Christian. Even then the idea of eternity seemed right to me. It was, and still is, my way of coping. To get through life's hard stuff.

And now that I am saved and born again. Now that I have everlasting life with Him. It is a solid truth. And it helps to try and understand all of the evil and pain in this world. Because it will not last. It is not even real, in a sense. In other words, once we are in heaven for eternity, this will all seem like such a short and mostly unimportant thing.

This short life we have is...................

2 Corinthians 4: 17 For our light affliction, which is but for a moment, is working for us a far more exceeding and eternal weight of glory,

It is for a moment. I know it seems like that is a lie, that your suffering continues sometimes for years at a time. But compared with the glory that is to come. Well, here is a picture I used for the VBS in the Philippines in 2019:

Let's say that this box represents your life. (then I have one of the kids get into this large cardboard box) this is your life maybe 75 or 90 years. But this room and this ocean and this Island, this whole world and the stars and all, that is eternity. That is where you will spend your life if you are His. Compared to this box here. You see, no matter how nice or bad that box may be, it is small and honestly so brief, compared to the universe.

How then can we survive the hard stuff? Well two verse come to mind:

Hebrews 13:5 Let your conduct be without covetousness; be content with such things as you have. For He Himself has said, "I will never leave you nor forsake you." 6 So we may boldly say: "The Lord is my helper. I will not fear. What can man do to me?"
The author of Hebrews is quoting Deuteronomy here (31:6)
And the other one is
John 16: 33 These things I have spoken to you, that in Me you may have peace. In the world you will have tribulation; but be of good cheer, I have overcome the world."

If you are or become His, then He will never forsake you and He wants you to be of good cheer. Because He has overcome this world, and with Him in you, so can you.
Again, this triggers a few more scriptures

from **Revelation Chapter 2:**
7 "He who has an ear, let him hear what the Spirit says to the churches. To him who overcomes I will give to eat from the tree of life, which is in the midst of the Paradise of God."
11 "He who has an ear, let him hear what the Spirit says to the churches. He who overcomes shall not be hurt by the second death."
17 "He who has an ear, let him hear what the Spirit says to the churches. To him who overcomes I will give some of the hidden manna to eat. And I will give him a white stone, and on the stone a new name written which no one knows except him who receives it." '
26 And he who overcomes, and keeps My works until the end, to him I will give power over the nations—
God calls us to be overcomers. To overcome these trials and temptations. And then, being a just and fair God, He gives us the power to do so. By abiding in Him we are then empowered to follow .....so the bad stuff is actually going to turn into good. If we just hang onto Him as He hangs unto us.

And then there are these verses:

James 1: 2 My brethren, count it all joy when you fall into various trials, 3 knowing that the testing of your faith produces patience. 4 But let patience have its perfect work, that you may be perfect and complete, lacking nothing

When we go through the trials of life, they will produce in is a perfection.

Not a pure sinless person, not in this life. The perfection means complete in Him.

Its one of my main themes that I have been talking about for these many years (to whoever might listen)

God has an abundant life for you

That life is to fulfill His purpose for you

That purpose it two-fold

1. To be conformed to His image **(Romans 8:29)**

2. To do those works that He set aside for you to do (you know before he created this universe, He had already set aside this abundant life for you) **(Ephesians 2:10)**

All we need do is abide, wait, and follow Him.

He will do the rest.

Be Blessed in Him Today

Philippine Bible Ministry

NOT CALLED TO SIN

Jeremiah 7: 8 "Behold, you trust in lying words that cannot profit. 9 Will you steal, murder, commit adultery, swear falsely, burn incense to Baal, and walk after other gods whom you do not know, 10 and then come and stand before Me in this house which is called by My name, and say, 'We are delivered to do all these abominations'? 11 Has this house, which is called by My name, become a den of thieves in your eyes? Behold, I, even I, have seen it," says the Lord.

In the days of Jeremiah, the people of God had forsaken the one true God and had added false idols to their worship, while at the same time they would come to the temple and call on the name of the Lord.

God would have none of it and would eventually destroy Jerusalem and the temple of Solomon and bring both Israel and Judah into captivity. Because they turned form actually following the God, they knew to be true. They were led astray by the things and the ideas of this world.

Whenever you begin to talk about the blessings and cursing of the Lord, it inevitably turns to a discussion on legalism.

Are we not free in Christ? those people back then were of course under the law; But more importantly than that, they were, much as His people today are, to follow the Lord.

The idea that we as Christians need not follow Him that we can just do our own thing and then He will bless us. This is insanity. Yet it is predominant in the Church world today.

Do you know anyone in church that still lives the same life as before they were "saved" That seem to be as greedy for money, for expensive things desiring to improve their physical lives all the time? Though they talk about serving Him, there is no evidence in their lives that they do.

Question for you; if you are not asking yourself daily how you may serve Him, but instead asking Him to bless whatever you want; Then is He your Lord? Or is He merely your friend that happens to offer salvation and self-fulfillment.

The prophet Jeremiah led an incredibly sad lonely life. No one followed him, except for his scribe; Baruk. Would that we all had a faithful Baruk in our walk.

To lead the life of the one that gives the word of truth to a fallen or falling or sleeping church; that is not a life that many would choose. It will not fill churches; nobody wants to hear about honoring Christ in their lives today.

They just want to be blessed, to enjoy their life, to have comforts, to be rescued from the upcoming tribulation. You get my point.

We do have freedom in Christ, but it does not mean what you think it means. It means freedom from sin, not freedom to sin.

"Christianity is not a sinning religion" Ravenhill once said. I know we do not like that word religion, so ok Christianity is not a sinning relationship. God came and lived as man and was crucified so that you could live a good life, a life free from sin; maybe not 100% of the time, but moment by moment our goal is to live in Him and if we do that, then we cannot sin.

The church is full of folks that love the emotions of the music, the comfort of or maybe the idea of His undying love. That is good, God is love. But you must try and understand that love is not this gooey soft thing that you might think it is. Love (sometimes, or for me often is) a swift kick in the pants to wake me and make me. To break me and make me.

Love is Christ on the Cross. Love is you surrendering your very life to Him. This will probably be uncomfortable at times. God works with humans and we usually require much stretching to become what He wants us to be.

Yes He will comfort you and heal you and touch you in amazing ways, ways which will make His love constrain you. That constraint from the Living God, should put you on your knees where you will trust Him with your life. Instead of just kind of rolling through life you may just start to live for Him

But He is a gentleman, He will never force you to comply. But if you do, you will find the best life. You will be able to say with the Psalmist:

Psalm 63:1 O God, you are my God; Early will I seek You; My soul thirsts for You; My flesh longs for You In a dry and thirsty land Where there is no water.

And when He gives you that living water you will be set free. Free to follow Him. To do His will.

Be Blessed in Him Today
Philippine Bible Ministry

NO LONGER SLAVES TO WHAT?

Popular worship song is called   No Longer Slaves (Bethel Music, 2015)

The song is about how we are no longer slaves to fear, because we are children of God

True enough, now that we have the Lord as our Father, we no longer need to be driven by fear

Verse do not fear what man can do

Psalm 118:6 The LORD is on my side; I will not fear. What can man do to me?

However, is that a scriptural song? Is it the bottom line about slavery for the Christian?

Do you ever stop and think on the words to these songs? Do you just run with your feelings, that it makes you feel good? A lot of today's worship songs are based on feelings and are more about our feelings than about actually touching the Lord or more importantly being touched by Him. The feelings in much of modern worship songs is about us, our feelings, our weakness, etc.. Not about Him

I love the melody of this song, I learned it on my guitar. I love to sing it.

But; the words are always sticking to my mind, because I know of a section of scripture that actually talks of being a slave. And it is more profound that just being about fear.

Romans 6:18 And having been set free from sin, you became slaves of righteousness.

Slaves to Christ, that is much more profound.

We are called to be holy and these verses, are about How we are now free not to sin.
But it is amazing that we are no longer slaves to sir, No longer searching for sin;, now we are free men and women
 Is it ok if I change the words in that song?
"I'm no longer a slave to sin
I am a slave to Christ"

Be Blessed in Him Today
Philippine Bible Ministry.

REDEEM YOUR TIME

Oswald Chambers:
"Our greatest fear is not that we will be damned, but that somehow Jesus Christ will be defeated. Also, our fear is that the very things our Lord stood for— love, justice, forgiveness, and kindness among men— will not win out in the end and will represent an unattainable goal for us. Then there is the call to spiritual perseverance. A call not to hang on and do nothing, but to work deliberately, knowing with certainty that God will never be defeated.
If our hopes seem to be experiencing disappointment right now, it simply means that they are being purified. Every hope or dream of the human mind will be fulfilled if it is noble and of God. But one of the greatest stresses in life is the stress of waiting for God. He brings ful- fillment, "because you have kept My command to persevere..." (Revela- tion 3:10)."

Today I just want to jump off of this daily Oswald devotional

These days I am very much thinking on how the Revival vs Rap- ture options that seem to be confronting the Western Church today.

I say Western Church, because these types of non-essentials are not much addressed in the rest of the world. They are too busy about the things that the Lord commands us. Salvation for the lost and Sanctification for the saved. They are living that dynamic vibrant life in Christ, that we in our comfortable West- ern culture cannot fully grasp.

So, adding to this idea of Revival or Rapture is another one on the same lines. It is comfort or hardship; which is truly the blessing?

For most church attending Christians in the USA, these seem like silly things to think upon. But are they really?

Track this with me for a second. If Jesus were with us today, do you think He would approve of your home church? You know the things that you are doing as a body, the things that are spending time on as believers. its not some works idea, but we are to be about His business.

Are we spending much time in serious prayer for the 1.5 million each week (I thought it was like a million, but a brother recently showed me some statistics that suggest its like 250,000 persons per day) that are going to damnation? No way out of Hell for them. Do you think that is priority one at our churches?

Or is priority one, looking for the Anti-Christ?

Or is it turning your church into a Jewish temple or Tabernacle and celebrating the Jewish Holy Days?

Or maybe a preoccupation with Israel?

Sorry to say that we may have our hearts turned off to the things that break His heart.

Jesus died for the sinners. That is our priority and to live for HIM!!

One more thought to think on: If the Lord did come today, do you think He would want this lukewarm passive comfortable thing we call Church?

Would it be amazing if the churches in China and Iran were the ones raptured and most of the Americans were left wondering what just happened?

Who is the church that Jesus spits out of His mouth?

I am praying it is not America.
I am kind of pleading with you here.
But I understand if you do not want to be challenged on this.
After all there must be some great Prophecy seminar in Israel this week

By the way, I am with Oswald on this, I do believe that God will pour out His Spirit on this world and that He will win. And then the end.

I am standing with Him persevering on this thought.

Matthew 24: 12 And because lawlessness will abound, the love of many will grow cold. 13 But he who endures to the end shall be saved.

We need to love our enemies and pray for them and see them saved, we need to endure or persevere on this idea. Yes?

Be Blessed in Him Today

Philippine Bible Ministry

HOLINESS AND HUMBLENESS

The Publican and the Pharisee

Many Christians believe that personal holiness and personal humbleness are opposites.

They are not, they are in point of fact two sides to a biblical coin.

Looking at the prayers of the Publican and the Pharisee in Luke 18 is where we often camp when we accuse those that say they believe in Holiness doctrines of being legalistic and pharisaical.

Luke 18 **¹⁰ "Two men went up to the temple to pray, one a Pharisee and the other a tax collector. ¹¹ The Pharisee stood and prayed thus with himself, 'God, I thank You that I am not like other men—extortioners, unjust, adulterers, or even as this tax collector. ¹² I fast twice a week; I give tithes of all that I possess.' ¹³ And the tax collector, standing afar off, would not so much as raise his eyes to heaven, but beat his breast, saying, 'God, be merciful to me a sinner!' ¹⁴ I tell you, this man went down to his house justified rather than the other; for everyone who exalts himself will be humbled, and he who humbles himself will be exalted."**

The truth of the matter is that this Pharisee suffered from self righteousness. This guy believed that he was holy because of what he either did or did not do. That is false, of course, and why? Because this man was speaking of his flesh, in fact , both men were speaking of their flesh,

The Publican (tax collector) very much knew that he was living in sin, and therefore his prayers to God were heard, because they were genuine, this man sought God's forgiveness.

God loves a humble and contrite heart, and this is actually the basis for our Holiness. It is to be humble, to realize just how horrible we are in our natural person. But of note here is that this publican guy was NOT SAVED, not at that point, perhaps he was on his way, the parable was a story not an actual event, meant to teach.

The difference with us, is that we are new creations in Him. The humbleness is about ourselves without Christ, **"oh wretched man that I am" (Romans 7)**,, but Christ comes and then we have this holiness dwelling in us. But it will never be activated until we let go and let God do this. It is His holiness, living in us, trying to get out and work through our humble and contrite new selves.

Yes, anyone that believes that following rules and not sinning will earn you any standing in Him is off, but do not be fooled. Doing or you might better say, obeying Jesus many commands to be holy, that is done in Him and through our broken selves.

That is not believing that we are better than anyone else. In face in many ways the person that is walking in Him knows better than anyone else that they are probably worse than the other one.

But you probably will thank God that you are not still

living and walking in life as a sinner every day.

That by Gods ace, mercy love you are able to walk in Him every day. In humbleness and yes most of the time, in holiness…(its not a bad word, holiness, its Gods amazing grace at work in our lives) if and as we stay humble.

*I will let the words of EM Bounds
close this post out today*

"*The pride of doing sends its poison all through our praying. The pride of being (on our own) infects all of our prayers, no matter how beautiful the words may be. This lack of humility, this self-applauding, this self-exaltation, kept the most religious man of Christ's day from being accepted by God. The same thing will keep us in this day from being accepted by Him" from EM Bounds, The Essentials of Prayer.*

Be Blessed in Him Today
Philippine Bible Ministry

WHAT ABOUT WORKS?

James said that "faith without works is dead"

What kind of works should we be about? Here are a few

2 Peter 1:5-8

But also for this very reason, giving all diligence, add to your faith virtue, to virtue knowledge, to knowledge self-control, to self-control perseverance, to perseverance godliness, to godliness brotherly kindness, and to brotherly kindness love. For if these things are yours and abound, you will be neither barren nor unfruitful in the knowledge of our Lord Jesus Christ.

<u>Christianity is not passive it is to be active</u>

Are we Disciples or are we merely saved? Is there a distinction between being saved and belonging to Him?

Jesus said that if you love Him you will obey Him

He was clear in that, how many times did Jesus tell us to follow Him, to put off the Old Man and to walk Holy in Him?

And to walk wholly in Him. (AND HOLY ALSO)

WE often think that the normal Western Christian way is enough, You might not have thought of this, you know, you were saved and then you go to church, and then you give a little, pray a little. You must be good to go see you one day saved in heaven, well done

I often think that maybe it is just me? Maybe I am reading this book wrong? Maybe there are just a few crazy folks out there that were more sold out than the rest?

Maybe we do not really need to take up our cross and follow Him? What did some of those folks say about Christianity? and what did Jesus say about being His disciple?

Amy Carmichael she was an amazing missionary with no fear, how did she feel about the church of her day
"The world has far too many runoff-the-ill Christians;cool, respectable, satisfied with the usual, the mediocre. Why bother laying ones life to multiply the number of those saved? Damascus blades is what we need, born in the fire of extremes that is what India needs.".
She was willing to pay the price. Do you think she was too radical? Or do you think she was just what the Lord had in mind for all His children?

Just so you know, if you are saved you will be His disciple, it is not an option. Those that love Him obey Him, or follow Him. It is not some kind of works thing, it is some kind of Jesus thing Look at these verses:

Matthew 16:24 Then Jesus said to His disciples, "If anyone desires to come after Me, let him deny himself, and take up his cross, and follow Me.
Matthew 8:19-20 Then a scribe came and said to Him, "Teacher, I will follow You wherever You go." Jesus said to him, "The foxes have holes and the birds of the air have nests, but the Son of Man has nowhere to lay His head."
Luke 9:59-60 And He said to another, "Follow Me." But he said, "Lord, permit me first to go and bury my father." But He said to him, "Allow the dead to bury their own dead; but as for you, go and proclaim everywhere the kingdom of God."
2 Corinthian 5:15 and He died for all, so that they who live might no longer live for themselves, but for Him who died and rose again on their behalf.
Galatians 2:20 "I have been crucified with Christ; and it is no longer I who live, but Christ lives in me; and the life which I now live in the flesh I live by faith in the Son of God, who loved me and gave Himself up for me.

In Jesus we must deny our own lives to follow Him. Those before who "gave it all up" to follow Him are just the normal Christ followers. That is what life in Him is it's not radical to Jesus.

THIS IS WHY THE FIRST CENTURY CHURCH WAS UNSTOPPABLE. THIS IS WHY FOLKS LIKE HUDSON TAYLOR, GEORGE MUELLER AND AMY CARMICHAEL WERE UNSTOPPABLE. THIS IS WHY THOSE IN THE UNDERGROUND CHINESE CHURCH ARE UNSTOPPABLE

THIS IS WHY I CRY OUT FOR REVIVAL. IN THE END YOUR LITTLE COMFORTABLE LIFE HERE MAY NOT MATTER MUCH, IF GOD IS CALLING YOU TO MORE!!!

Matthew 19 21 Jesus said to him, "If you want to be perfect, go, sell what you have and give to the poor, and you will have treasure in heaven; and come, follow Me."22 But when the young man heard that saying, he went away sorrowful, for he had great possessions.

I used to believe that the rich young ruler was somebody else, not me, someone else that struggled with possessions, not me. But it slowly began to dawn on me, that I am that rich young ruler. You know living in the USA I am that rich young ruler,
Ill I go away sorrowful or will I sell all and follow Him.
If you still do not believe me, I suggest you try and find a way around this verse.

Luke 1433 So likewise, whoever of you does not forsake all that he has cannot be My disciple.
This is not a metaphor for how we are controlled by our possessions, this is the truth of the gospel
I am telling you this one thing; If you all do this; If you give it up and live for Him.
Then He will bless you beyond measure
If even a few thousand folks do this worldwide
This world will be turned upside down, or right side up actually
Just like it was in the first century by those disciples/

Joshua 24:15 And if it seems evil to you to serve the LORD, choose for yourselves this day whom you will serve, whether the gods which your fathers served that were on the other side of

the River, or the gods of the Amorites, in whose land you dwell. But as for me and my house, we will serve the LORD.

Be Blessed in Him Today
Philippine Bible Ministry

CHALLENGED OR CHANGED

"The question isn't:' were you challenged?' The question is;' were you changed?" Leonard Ravenhill

We all love to hear challenging sermons. Real cutting-edge stuff that stirs us up. The stuff that motivates us to change. It pumps us up for a while, but the real question is," does it change us?"
All the good intention in a challenge is useless when there is no outcome; or as Michael W Smith said in one of his songs," *The road to good intentions doesn't lead you anywhere*" It in fact leads you to hell. Because, without any change (or regeneration) there is no Jesus. Or do you think that Jesus and faith are just some kind of cool thing to say? you know just some prayer you made one day, that really did not seem to change anything? If you have seen no change in your life, then I would warn you of this verse:

2 Corinthians 5:17 Therefore, if anyone is in Christ, he is a new creation; old things have passed away; behold, all things have become new.

This means that if you are not changed, then you are not in Christ, then you are not saved.
One of my former pastors would often say that, "lots of people say a lots of things". Meaning a lot of folks say a lot of things, but what matters is not so much what they say as what they do.

Matthew 21: 28 "But what do you think? A man had two sons, and he came to the first and said, 'Son, go, work today in my vineyard.' 29 He answered and said, 'I will not,' but afterward he regretted it and went. 30 Then he came to the second and said likewise. And he answered and said, 'I go, sir,' but he did not go. 31 Which of the two did the will of his father?" They said to Him,

"The first."

The one who does the Fathers will is the one that is the true son , the saved one.

Jesus said, "For whoever does the will of My Father in heaven is My brother and sister and mother." Matthew 12:50

because faith is an action word. It is not a feeling nor emotion, it is not just about your mental state. Not something that you think is true. In fact, true faith has to be attached to something and acted upon, or else it is more like a wish.

Faith must be in something that is real, like God for example. Faith in faith is just pretending.
Faith, that gift from the Lord, leads to salvation, which of course changes people. It gives us the ability not to sin, it changes our direction from running away from God to running towards Him
Once we are changed by Him, then all who know us can see it by our actions.
Good sermons, the ones that convict us and lead to our repentance, those actually change us.
The other ones, well they might pump us up for a week or two, but in the end we are the same old person.

We are saved, not only from hell, but saved from sin, saved to be a new creation.
Just so, the one who is actually changed, whose life shows that they are different, that one is saved.
Not the one that is challenged to be changed, they are only challenged. They actually have no faith.

Be Blessed in Him Today
Philippine Bible Ministry

BURN THE BOATS

Acts 27:32 Then the soldiers cut away the ropes of the skiff and let it fall off.

During a raging storm (Acts 27) Paul convinced the crew to release the small boat that they would have used to save themselves from almost certain death as the ship was about to crash on the rocks. They had faith in Paul. They all lived even though the ship was destroyed.
Good thing for them that Paul's Faith was in God.

Back in the Middle Ages when Vikings wanted to colonize new territory; the first thing they did was to burn the boats after they arrived. Sealing their fate to either survive or perish in this new land.
You might call it an act of faith in their ability to survive.

Faith in themselves. That is what the world teaches.
The works teaches that we all have some kind of amazing power in our own heart. You don't need God, because you can ultimately make your own way. Pull yourself up by your bootstraps, as it were.
That is part of the heritage of Americans. Man, it sounds good. Too bad it is one of the enemies' best tactics to keep folks away from Jesus: Self-reliance.

Anyone that has ever stumbled, fallen into depression or addiction or something else that they feel powerless against will tell you that they never found this magical power. Even in the 12 steps they say that it is the higher power (which i call God) that heals.

Psalm 138:8 (a) The Lord will perfect that which concerns me;

Trust in Him and He will take care of your concerns.
Sometimes He won't remove that thing. But He promises to give you the way to live with it.

2 Corinthians 12:19 And He said to me, "My grace is sufficient for you, for My strength is made perfect in weakness." Therefore, most gladly I will rather boast in my infirmities, that the power of Christ may rest upon me

If He doesn't remove your affliction He will change you. That power that we all seek within our natural selves is available in our "born again", new selves.
In the end every human will let you down, even yourself.

(If you see someone that claims to be a Christian but always brags about their ability. Well, those are not the leaders you should follow.)

Be Blessed in Him Today
Philippine Bible Ministry

RENEWING OF
THE MIND

Ephesians 4: ²² that you put off, concerning your former conduct, the old man which grows corrupt according to the deceitful lusts, ²³ and be renewed in the spirit of your mind,

These verses are right below the ones that speak of the Church someday growing up into unity, by the gifts of the ministers of the gospel and the body of Christ.This renewing of the mind in the Sprit is what I would call an essential doctrine for sanctification. How are we to do this?

This renewing or the mind will cause the new creation, that born again self, to take control of our very lives. This is the root of the abundant life that Jesus promised for His disciples. Which, I believe, all true believers are.

One way that we renew our mind is by the washing of the word. The vbery next chapter Ephesians 5 we see these verses:

Eph 5:25-26 ²⁵ Husbands, love your wives, just as Christ also loved the church and gave Himself for her, ²⁶ that He might [g] sanctify and cleanse her with the washing of water by the word,

The Lord sanctifies and cleanses wives by the word of God; the Bible. It stands to reason that all of us are likewise cleansed and sanctified. I would say we are revived and renewed by reading and studying our Bibles.

2 Timothy 3: ¹⁶ All Scripture is given by inspiration of God, and is profitable for doctrine, for reproof, for correction, for [c]instruction in righteousness, ¹⁷ that the man of God may be complete,

thoroughly equipped for every good work.

Interesting verse here, it says that the Bible is profitable to complete the man of God to be 100% equipped to do the good works of the Lord; in other words: the Bible equips us to be disciples of Christ.

Here is another verse about the renewing of the mind:

Romans 12: I beseech you therefore, brethren, by the mercies of God, that you present your bodies a living sacrifice, holy, acceptable to God, which is your [reasonable service. ² And do not be conformed to this world, but be transformed by the renewing of your mind, that you may prove what is that good and acceptable and perfect will of God.

Again this renewing of the mind, is what assists in that transformation into that new creation that Jesus brings to life in us at the point of salvation.

We have seen that one way to do this is the Bible.

The Bible is not what many think it is. It is not a book of rules and regulations that holds mysteries that will unlock some kind of power that you can use.

It is in fact a living book. It is in fact a very spiritual book, that seems to change with each reading. No one can ever fully grasp all that it contains.

Though many millions have been converted by reading their Bibles, it is in fact a book that cannot be understood unless one is born again with the Holy Spirit indwelling, guiding, and teaching us the things that God wants us to learn.

There is a simplicity to it, yet it is also a book of more layers than any onion

The Bible also will not change anyone that does not approach it with the proper thought and attitude.

Without going into depth, the basic idea is to approach the Bible with prayer and asking Him to lead and teach you.

Pray before you read and ask for His guidance. However, one reads their Bible, I suggest that you read it all the way through, many times. I suggest that you learn it inside and out. Not necessarily to memorize the whole thing, but some like Hank Hanegraaff and

David Hocking are able to memorize whole books of the Bible. But for me it is more about having the ideas and several power verses in your "heart" this way you know what it says, it helps so that you do not get led astray down these side eddies that some pastors or teachers like to go down (aka rabbit holes).

But a thorough, prayerful journey through Gods word will change you. It will transform your mind and allow you to put on the new man

Matthew 4:4 But He answered and said, "It is written, 'Man shall not live by bread alone, but by every word that proceeds from the mouth of God.' "

Colossians 3:-9 Do not lie to one another, since you have put off the old man with his deeds, 10 and have put on the new man who is renewed in knowledge according to the image of Him who created him,

Here are some quotes about the Bible:

Immanuel Kant (1724-1804) said: "The existence of the Bible, as a book for the people, is the greatest benefit which the human race has ever experienced. Every attempt to belittle it is a crime against humanity."

Horace Greeley (1811-1872), "It is impossible to mentally or socially enslave a Bible-reading people."

George Washington, "It is impossible to rightly govern the world without God and the Bible."

Be Blessed in Him Today

Philippine Bible Ministry

FAILURES AND LOSS/ AMAZING LOVE

James 1:2 My brethren, count it all joy when ye fall into diverse temptations, 3 knowing this: that the trying of your faith worketh patience. 4 But let patience have her perfect work, that ye may be perfect and entire, lacking nothing.

Recently I saw a question on a Christian page on Facebook. The question; is it OK to be mad at God? As I have experience in this topic, I was glad to have an answer. Being mad at God is not the sign of lack of faith or because the Bible tells us not to. Instead, it was real life stuff. And therefore, it carries more power and weight than mere head knowledge does.

Yes, the scripture is true, and the word of God is powerful, But He also takes us through a lot of stuff so that He can use us, and for me so that He can protect me from myself.

This idea of anger towards God; Let me tell you a bit of my story: I was once a Bible and Social Studies teacher at a Christian School. It was so amazing, I wound up presenting most of our Friday Chapel services, which were in essence Topical Sermons, meant to challenge and touch the lives of our 7-12th grade students. I was so blessed. The Principal/Owner of the school wanted to buy a church, for our school, and also for Sunday Services for at risk youth. He envisioned me as a Pastor there in some capacity.

I felt like I had finally arrived. I had been wanting this position, to be a Pastor, every since I was first saved in 1993 at the age of 37.

Also, at this time I was attending a solid Bible Teaching Calvary Chapel Church, very involved in a Saturday Men's Bible study. I had my marriage to my Christian wife and my beautiful little daughter.

But God had other plans. The school closed first, so I had to go back to school, work two part time jobs, etc. My marriage ended, taking my young daughter to another state. I was about to lose my house, so we sold it.

I was so angry with God. How could He take all this away? All I was trying to do was to serve Him. Wasn't it His will to be in these ministries and this marriage?

No time for the whole story here, But as I poured out my anger and my hurt to Him. You know what He did? He just listened and picked me up, held me and loved me. Where else could I go? He is now and always will be my God and My Savior. These events went into shaping me for the ministries that I am now in. And it taught me to trust in Him. Not in my circumstance.

By the way, I no longer need to be called a Pastor; Brother Dave will do just fine

Be Blessed in Him Today
Philippine Bible Ministry

WHAT DO WE GIVE THE LORD?

Jesus gave His life for us on the cross. He came to earth made himself into a servant and suffered for us. What do we give Him in return?

Not for our salvation, nothing we can give for that it was settled at the cross. No, this is about our life as a believer. What is our response to His gift? Besides gratitude, love, etc.? Our sins?

The Lord does not want your nasty old sins. He wants you.

He takes our sins and forgives us. But is that all we give Him? Is that all there is to it?

No, He wants you, all of you Sacrificed on the altar

Romans 12:1 I beseech you therefore, brethren, by the mercies of God, that you present your bodies a living sacrifice, holy, acceptable to God, which is your reasonable service.

Your body here is your flesh, your physical and emotional life. pretty much everything of you that is not of Him. And when God pours out His Fire. It is then that we are burnt on that altar. It's the sacrifice that is burnt up. Not the altar. John the Baptist spoke of Jesus and the coming baptism by fire when he said in

Matthew 3:11 11 I indeed baptize you with water unto repentance, but He who is coming after me is mightier than I, whose sandals I am not worthy to carry. He will baptize you with the Holy Spirit and fire.

Your rights, your comforts, your desires. All of it burned up there by and for Him

Not that we all need to give all of our possessions to Him, but we all should be more than WILLING to do what Jesus asked the Rich Young Ruler to do

Luke 18:22So when Jesus heard these things, He said to him, "You still lack one thing. Sell all that you have and distribute to the poor, and you will have treasure in heaven; and come, follow Me."

Then what is left? Well what is left is what He gives us.

A new heart.

A soft heart

Ezekiel 11:10 Then I will give them one heart, and I will put a new spirit within them, and take the stony heart out of their flesh, and give them a heart of flesh,

Then that new soft heart will be in His will, and then He will give us the right desires, His desires:

Psalm 37:4 Delight yourself also in the Lord, And He shall give you the desires of your heart.

It takes a lot to get us to that Abraham place.

By faith Abraham, when he was tested, offered up Isaac, and he who had received the promises offered up his only begotten son,

Offered that son that he waited 100 years for, offered him up to be slain, in total surrender.

That place of total surrender to sacrifice the one you love. which is yourself of course.

The Lord did not take Isaac from Abraham, but the man's faith was complete in this act.

The Lord will take your flesh and then your faith will also be complete

This is one way that God tests your faith

to see if you are ready to lay it all out, to put your family, spouse, children, everything on that altar than comes the blessing

James 1:3 knowing that the testing of your faith produces patience. 4 But let patience have its perfect work, that you may be perfect and complete, lacking nothing

This is all part of that second blessing you may have heard about, the Sanctification available to those that are saved.

Be Blessed in Him Today
Philippine Bible Ministry

CLOSE ENCOUNTERS OF THE GOD KIND

What really changes a believer is when they have a close encounter with the Lord.

In the OT Temple they had the inner sanctuary, the Holy of Holies, where the High Priest only went in once a year. There was no light in this inner chamber, no candles. Nothing was needed because the Glory of the Lord illuminated it.

They said the priest face was shining after their encounter with God's presence. It is powerful, coming before the Living God. It undoes people, falling prostrate before Him, it will be a life changing event

it is not just an emotional response, where you feel His presence, like you just heard a really cool worship song. But then after the service, that feeling is gone, but it was cool, maybe it was His presence, or maybe it was your own emotions,

What happens is God gives you an opportunity, and then you need to surrender,

If you do not surrender to the vision, He gives you in those moments, then you will not have any change in your life. It becomes a missed opportunity.

Yield to the purposes of heaven and God will give you a vision; yield to the vision and God will make it happen, as you lean into him and,,, here is the kicker....MOVE OUT IN THAT VISION.

Don't tell Him to wait until you do this or that, Once He gets hold of you like that, once you have that awesome rare opportunity to be that close to Him, than you are a fool who would not do it.

If you look at the history makers in the Church, folks like, DL Moody, Charles Spurgeon, Amy Carmichael, Taylor Hudson, Leonard Ravenhill....They followed the unction of the Lord and they became History makers,

God is not done using surrendered vessels to make History, God will use you in some way that you cannot even imagine.

While many Christians limp through life, barely hanging on to Him, and seem to be stuck in phase one (Salvation) God is calling us to do great things, The book of Acts is still being written in some ways, God still wants to have a world wide Revival, And those that push into Him and get into that inner chamber are called to make History,

You might look at them, and then come up with so many excuses why that is not happening now.

We are not necessarily talking about the Acts of the original Apostles, But the acts of those History Makers.

Its not too much to think that God could be calling you to do great things.
1 Corinthians 1:27
But God has chosen the foolish things of the world to put to shame the wise, and God has chosen the weak things of the world to put to shame the things which are mighty;

God uses anyone that is available and surrendered to do His work.

Eternity is a long time to be without the rewards that God wants you to have.
This life is so short to use its comfort as an excuse not to do what God has created you to do

Pray about this

let's make History together in His name,

History is after all His Story.

Be Blessed in Him Today
Philippine Bible Ministry

RESOLUTION: TO BE HIS DISCIPLE.

To follow Him we need to know Him and to know Him means to read His words and then spend time alone with Him in prayer.

Simple way to read the Bible:
Read a chapter, then ask yourself "what does this say about God?" "What does this say about mankind?" And "What does this say to me?"

Romans 8:29 For whom He foreknew, He also predestined to be conformed to the image of His Son, that He might be the firstborn among many brethren

To be conformed to the Image of Christ, we must be disciples; This occurs by following Him. This begins by becoming humble; By submitting to one another (Other Christians) in HimAnd by reading His word, which is a good way to get to know Him.

These three things show the characteristic of a servant, which Jesus had and has the heart of the servant., so if we are to be conformed to His image, we need to have that servant's heart. Not the heart of a "leader" but the heart of a servant, who is then ASKED to lead, and asked by those being led, not be someone else.

This is that shepherd that the sheep know and trust to take care of them. .Let me be the one that serves others in humbleness. That is not my natural state, I need help to do this, and that help can only come from the Holy Spirit, from the Lord Himself.It is only when we surrender our very lives to Him that we can then learn this.

It is about doing things that you naturally would not want to do, because it is the right thing to do and more importantly it is the way that you already know Christ would want you to live.The cost may be high in terms of your perceived comfort and status. But the gain is unimaginable. It is the beginning of the abundant life that Christ has promised.

John 10:10 The thief does not come except to steal, and to kill, and to destroy. I have come that they may have life, and that they may have it more abundantly.

The thief is the devil, that rascal that pretty much rules this world, and the status and comfort that he offers you is meant to steal your joy, it is meant to steal your abundant life. That life is only yours as you follow Him. You may have some kinds of cool moments and even happiness, but you will not have that "abundant life" that Christ offers unless you follow Him.

I promise you that life is the best that could ever be, and will ever be yours for eternity, By the way, that is a long time.

Be Blessed in Him Today
Philippine Bible Ministry

NUMBER YOUR DAYS AND REDEEM YOUR TIME

Psalm 90:12 So teach us to number our days, That we may gain a heart of wisdom

Ephesians 5:16 redeeming the time, because the days are evil.

Colossians 4:5 Walk in wisdom toward those who are outside, redeeming the time.

Number - manah= {appoint} {count} {number} {prepare} {set} tell. to reckon

Redeem Greek:exagorazō

to make wise and sacred use of every opportunity for doing good, so that zeal and well doing are as it were the purchase money by which we make the time our own

We are to reckon that we have only so many days to live on earth, then we should make wise sacred use of the time the God gave us.

I am addicted to entertainment. I admit it. I grew up with the TV on all the time whether it was watched or not. I memorized the TV Guide. Our family gatherings the talk was about football and movies.

About 3 or 4 years ago my wife started to attempt to pull me away from this , my evening TV time was 3-4 hours. I never really thought about it much. But it started with my wife pointing out the stuff that honestly I should not be putting before my eyes.

Psalm 101: 3 I will set nothing wicked before my eyes;

Then the Lord began to work on me. Redeem your time, He kept telling me this over and over, "David you need to redeem your time for Me." This is very powerful to me, as I have sought in my heart to live for Him. At least that is what I told myself back in 1993 when I was saved. But was I really doing that, you know, actually living for Him. Or was He just a part, and maybe not such a big part, of my life.

Then I discovered this powerful old preacher Leonard Ravenhill Here is the sentence from him that still echoes in my heart this day, "Entertainment is the devils substitute for joy"

The enemy of my soul is Satan, and that guy wants to create something, anything, that will keep me from spending time with Jesus. Entertainment, it doesn't even need to be something vile, just something to waste your time on.

This does not mean that one cannot nor should not spend some down time , in fact it is healthy to do. But how much of my day, how much of your day, is spend on pursuits of nothing but entertainment.

The word amusement, means without thought, and that is just what comes from it, no thought, no good thing, no lasting thing anyway.

If you want to follow Him you should spend time with Him, Just like when you love someone you want to spend time with them. Its pretty simple really.

My goal for last year was to spend at least as much time in Christ as i do on other stuff

Goal met last year I spend at least as much time doing these things:

Bible reading

Bible study

Listening to sermons or good biblical teaching

listening to good Christian music

watching Christian movies (OK some of those are pretty much just entertainment, but some are amazingly uplifting)

Prayer

as I did watching sports, and superhero/action movies etc...

This year my goal is to spend more time with Him

and the main reason why is that it causes my love for Him to grow, it causes my desire and thirst for more of Him to grow, and it causes me to want to give more of my life and time to Him
So join me, if you will, Lets redeem our time in 2020
and see what God does with us.

Be Blessed in Him Today
Philippine Bible Ministry

ARE WE DISCIPLES OR ARE WE MERELY SAVED?

Is there a distinction between being saved and belonging to Him?
Jesus said that if you love Him you will obey Him.
How many times did Jesus tell us to follow Him; to put off the Old
Man and to walk Holy in Him? And to walk holy and wholly in
Him?

WE often think that the normal Western Christian way is enough,
you might not have thought of this, you know, you were saved
and then you go to church, and then you give a little, pray a little.
You must be good to go: see you one day saved in heaven, well
done.
I often think that maybe it is just me? Maybe I am reading this
book wrong? Maybe there are just a few crazy folks out there that
were more sold out than the rest?
Maybe we do not really need to take up our cross and follow Him?
What did some of those folks say about Christianity? and what
did Jesus say about being His disciple?

Amy Carmichael she was an amazing missionary who fearlessly
went to India by herself and did an amazing work, saving hundreds of children, in India. how did she feel about the church of
her day?
"The world has far too many run-of-the-mill Christians; cool, respectable, satisfied with the usual, the mediocre. Why bother lay-

ing one's life to multiply the number of those saved? Damascus blades is what we need, born in the fire of extremes that is what India needs.".

She was willing to pay the price. Do you think she was too radical? Or do you think her way is just what the Lord has in mind for all His children?

Just so you know, if you are saved you will be His disciple, it is really not an option. Those that love Him obey Him, or follow Him. It is not some kind of works thing; it is some kind of Jesus thing; Look at these verses:

Matthew 16: 24 Then Jesus said to His disciples, "If anyone desires to come after Me, let him deny himself, and take up his cross, and follow Me.

Matthew 8:19-20 Then a scribe came and said to Him, "Teacher, I will follow You wherever You go." Jesus said to him, "The foxes have holes and the birds of the air have nests, but the Son of Man has nowhere to lay His head."

Luke 9:59-60 And He said to another, "Follow Me." But he said, "Lord, permit me first to go and bury my father." But He said to him, "Allow the dead to bury their own dead; but as for you, go and proclaim everywhere the kingdom of God."

2 Corinthian 5:15 and He died for all, so that they who live might no longer live for themselves, but for Him who died and rose again on their behalf.

Galatians 2:20 "I have been crucified with Christ; and it is no longer I who live, but Christ lives in me; and the life which I now live in the flesh I live by faith in the Son of God, who loved me and gave Himself up for me.

In Jesus, we must deny our own lives to follow Him. Those before who "gave it all up" to follow Him are just the normal Christ followers. That is what life in Him that is the normal Christian life. THIS IS WHY THE FIRST CENTURY CHURCH WAS UNSTOPPABLE. THIS IS WHY FOLKS LIKE HUDSON TAYLOR, GEORGE MUELLER AND AMY CARMICHAEL WERE UNSTOPPABLE. THIS IS WHY

THOSE IN THE UNDERGROUND CHINESE CHURCH ARE UNSTOP-
PABLE
THIS IS WHY I CRY OUT FOR REVIVAL. IN THE END YOUR LITTLE
COMFORTABLE LIFE HERE MAY NOT MATTER MUCH, IF GOD IS
CALLING YOU TO MORE!!!

**Matthew 19 21 Jesus said to him, "If you want to be perfect, go,
sell what you have and give to the poor, and you will have treasure in heaven; and come, follow Me."22 But when the young man
heard that saying, he went away sorrowful, for he had great possessions.**

I used to believe that the rich young ruler was somebody else, not
me, someone else that struggled with possessions, not me. But it
slowly began to dawn on me, that I am that rich young ruler. You
know living in the USA I am that rich young ruler,
Ill I go away sorrowful or will I sell all and follow Him.
If you still do not believe me, I suggest you try and find a way
around this verse.

**Luke 14:33 So likewise, whoever of you does not forsake all that
he has cannot be My disciple.**
**This is not a metaphor for how we are controlled by our posses-
sions, this is the truth of the gospel**

I am telling you this one thing; If you all do this,If you give it up
and live for Him
He will bless you beyond measure.
If even a few thousand folks do this worldwide then this world
will be turned upside down , or right side up actually. Just like it
was in the first century by those disciples:

**Joshua 24:15 And if it seems evil to you to serve the LORD,
choose for yourselves this day whom you will serve, whether
the gods which your fathers served that were on the other side of
the River, or the gods of the Amorites, in whose land you dwell.
But as for me and my house, we will serve the LORD.**

DAVID PINSON

Be Blessed in Him Today
Philippine Bible Ministry

REDEEM YOUR TIME

<u>Oswald Chambers:</u>
<u>"Our greatest fear is not that we will be damned, but that somehow</u>
<u>Jesus Christ will be defeated. Also, our fear is that the very things our</u>
<u>Lord stood for— love, justice, forgiveness, and kindness among men—</u>
<u>will not win out in the end and will represent an unattainable goal for</u>
<u>us. Then there is the call to spiritual perseverance. A call not to hang</u>
<u>on and do nothing, but to work deliberately, knowing with certainty</u>
<u>that God will never be defeated. If our hopes seem to be experiencing</u>
<u>disappointment right now, it simply means that they are being puri-</u>
<u>fied. Every hope or dream of the human mind will be fulfilled if it is</u>
<u>noble and of God. But one of the greatest stresses in life is the stress</u>
<u>of waiting for God. He brings fulfillment,</u> **"because you have kept My**
command to persevere…" (Revelation 3:1<u>0</u>)."

Today I just want to jump off of this daily Oswald devotional
These days I am very much thinking on how the Revival vs Rapture options that seem to be confronting the Western Church today.

I say Western Church, because these types of non-essentials are not much addressed in the rest of the world. They are too busy about the things that the Lord commands us. Salvation for the lost and Sanctification for the saved. They are living that dynamic vibrant life in Christ, that we in our comfortable Western culture cannot fully grasp.

So adding to this idea of Revival or Rapture is another one on the same lines. It is comfort or hardship; which is truly the blessing?

For most church attending Christians in the USA, these seem like silly things to think upon. But are they really?

Track this with me for a second. If Jesus were with us today, do you think He would approve of your home church? You know the things that you are doing as a body, the things that are spending time on as believers. it's not some works idea, but we are to be about His business.

Are we spending much time in serious prayer for the 1.5 million each week (I thought it was like a million, but a brother recently showed me some statistics that suggest its like 250,000 persons per day) that are going to damnation?. Do you think that is a priority at our churches?

Or is priority one, looking for the Anti-Christ? Or is it turning your church into a Jewish temple or Tabernacle and celebrating the Jewish Holy Days? Or maybe a preoccupation with Israel?

Sorry to say that we may have our hearts turned off to the things that break His heart.

Jesus died for the sinners. That is our priority and to live with and for HIM!!

One more thought to think on: If the Lord did come today, do you think He would want this lukewarm passive comfortable thing we call Church?

Would it be amazing if the churches in China and Iran were the ones raptured and most of the Americans were left wondering what just happened?

Who is the church that Jesus spits out of His mouth?

I am praying it is not America. I am kind of pleading with you here.

But I understand if you do not want to be challenged on this.

After all there must be some great Prophecy seminar in Israel this week

By the way, I am with Oswald on this, I do believe that God will pour out His Spirit on this world and that He will win. And then the end.

I am standing with Him persevering on this thought.

Matthew 24: 12 And because lawlessness will abound, the love of many will grow cold. 13 But he who endures to the end shall be saved.

We need to love our enemies and pray for them and see them saved, we need to endure or persevere on this idea....

Yes?

Be Blessed in Him Today
Philippine Bible Ministry

Surrender your time to Him:

I know these days many of us seem to be "too busy" to do anything except to work and sleep.

That may be true, but I believe that we make time for the things that are important to us.

And I believe that the one who created us should be important.

Just think about it. Its not some kind of law to spend time in Him or in fellowship with His people, or doing His works,.

Its just that He wants you and your time.

And others are probably missing that Godly fellowship ,

And others are in need of that ministry that only you can provide.

Life is short and there is no do over button.

Redeem your time in Him

Please reach out to us

philippinebibleministry@gmail.com

BE BLESSED IN HIM TODAY

PHILIPPINE BIBLE MINISTRY

Made in the USA
Middletown, DE
24 February 2021